Baked in Pain

Baked in Pain

By
Amanda S. Dambuza

Your traumatic past may just be the fuel you need to soar

Professional typesetting by www.MYeBook.co.za

Dedication

I would like to dedicate this book firstly to an amazing God who saw fit to pick me for this jaw-dropping journey. To my mother for giving birth to me so that I could have a chance to fight for the life I have been able to build. To my husband, my life partner, my cheerleader and a great father. To my three children for being my inspiration, thank you for choosing me as your mother thereby giving me a chance to heal through you. Your un-conditional love gives me the wings to fly every day. To everyone out there who has ever faced insurmountable challenges and wondered if there is ever a time when they could just smile; this book is for you.

Table of Contents

Preface

The journeys people travel in life are defined by both what happened and what did not happen along the way. If people share similar experiences, empathy is possible, and the meaning people attached to these encounters can be shared and exchanged. If people share a communal language to describe events, and if connotations are similar, then the exchange of the message and meaning is possible. By sharing stories, people will validate each other's experiences, make pain and aspirations real. Empathy, understanding, and acceptance is possible, and a much deeper level of sensitivity can exist. Then, the story becomes understandable and not only endorses the experiences people had, but it authenticates their response to it.

But what happens if the story is foreign, and out of "sense-making reach" of those who are the recipients of the message? What happens if the language patterns used to describe things with and the connotations attached to those stories simply have no commonality? If the latter is true, then the exchange and "translation" of meaning and stories cannot happen, and the decoding of the messages become problematic.

With little to share, big gaps occur between the

meaning the storyteller wants to convey and the ability of the recipient to make sense of the story, its meaning and connotations. Consequently, people remain in isolated "meaning" bubbles where the exchanges are transactional and deep understanding and empathy is hardly possible.

If it was possible for me to listen to the story of an Eskimo of 1800, it will be close to impossible to have more than a transactional understanding. I might think that I understand certain things, but a deeper, more insightful understanding will be close to impossible. I certainly will not understand the connotations and deeper meanings. Empathy, understanding, and acceptance will be difficult, and a much deeper level of sensitivity cannot exist.

South Africa is a country where significantly different sets of experiences are the order of the day. The scenario as described in the previous paragraph is not only possible, but rather an every-day occurrence. It becomes quite easy for people with vastly different journeys to never really understand each other and to live in different worlds of meaning. Simply put, it is very difficult to "get" each other. It not only happens between people, but between groups in a community and society at large. The result is an ecosystem of tiers and bubbles where it is difficult to understand each other and where true empathy is hardly possible.

To break down the silos, tiers, and bubbles, we

have to spend time and energy – with a lot of positive intent – to listen to and explore each other's worlds. We should not listen with a predefined mindset, but rather be open to explore meaning completely outside of our frames of reference. We should be open to the fact that an event can be understood in vastly different ways.

In this book, Amanda Dambuza tells her story. Her story is honest, raw, often brutal. It is the naked honesty and courage that immediately overwhelms the reader. For me, as a white Afrikaner male growing up in a different tier and bubble, it resembles the theater of the absurd, where reality is much more bizarre than the most outrageous fiction. It awakens the senses through shock therapy that a parallel universe really existed in our beloved country. From my bubble, it is a universe where – in the penetrating words of Shakespeare – "foul is fair and fair is foul", where the universal people laws of gravity do not exist. My world and the world I knew of has little relation to the world Amanda shares.

By telling her story and by sharing her experiences, she makes it possible for people from a different bubble to start a journey of deeper understanding. Through her story, people who understand it – because they have shared experiences and attribute similar meaning to events and happenings – can authorise their own experiences. They can identify with the narrative and validate their emotions. The story of Amanda can then give hope to those who have been constrained by being on a similar journey, but perhaps had not the audacity to challenge what life gave them.

Amanda's journey is not a lullaby; a simple before-sleep read that dissociates one from the stark South African reality. It is not an escape – it is a confrontation. It is not a story of a Cinderella living happily ever after. It is not the murmuring of a self-referent motivational speaker, who wants to dispense a seven-step story on how to move from hardship to success.

Like looking at a Rorschach inkblot, we all have to find a distinctive truth in her story. A truth that speaks to each person as a segment of one. On one side, her story becomes a method and means for understanding so much more about the people of our country; on the other side, it validates and can provide hope.

Amanda, although playing herself in this book, is a metaphor and character in the story. By being the central character around which the story is weaved, we can identify with the person; yet, the story remains interpretable from the various points of view from which we experience it. It bursts through with truths that are as relevant to young girls growing up in townships as it does to middle-aged, white Afrikaner men.

Her story is a multi-layered cake. For me as an individual, it speaks to me about how her contrasting experiences can enhance and clarify my understanding of what happened in a parallel universe in the same country in which I live. It allows me to make sense of her experiences and to respond to her in more appropriate ways. Much more importantly though, we can generalise her experiences and become aware of how others think and feel based on their completely different journeys. As groups of people we can vastly increase our understanding and empathy, and become much more sensitive to the journeys of other groups. South Africa with its multiple tiers, bubbles, and strata has too many divides.

To overcome the divide, we all need to become translators who have a deeper understanding of the distinctly different journeys. People who can make sense of the range of stories and messages of the people of our country.... guides who can act as the go-between, between the bubbles and who can contribute to a much deeper understanding of each other.

The book makes one realise that it starts with people really wanting to understand the journeys of other people. In this case, we are provoked by the journey of Amanda to do so. One is also impelled to read it without a pre-formulated view, to suspend judgement, to immediately not attempt to make comparisons, and to understand that it is not a different version of your own truth, but rather a journey and truth of its own.

By pure anecdotal observation as individuals, we mostly have the savvy and the inclination to understand other individuals a bit better, to have less judgement and more empathy. But perhaps, as a group and as a nation, we are still far from it. On a collective level, we seem to forget or simply disregard that others may have a completely different take on things, thrust onto them by different journeys. Our empathy fails us when we become groups and we fall back on simplistic one-dimensional stereotypes. People are dehumanised and put into boxes from where we act belligerently to those people in other boxes. One hour of Twitter clearly demonstrates how easily we can fall apart. We far too easily forget about the stories of the many Amandas.

We see too much of it in business, politics, and social life. Headlines of racism, exclusion, bigotry, discrimination, and reverse discrimination displays an intolerance to develop a deeper, and more genuine understanding of the journeys the "others" have travelled.

By sharing our journeys, not only amongst those who are similar to us, but more importantly those we are dissimilar to, we deepen our understanding of each other, not only as individuals but as collectives. By understanding each other better, more empathy and sensitivity is possible. Nation building is possible, but only if we understand the different worlds we live in as South Africans. To get to know the stories of others and to realise that groups are merely the aggregate of many individual stories.

The story of Amanda is a story about the past, with much more relevance for the future. It is a story of hope, baked in the pain of one individual who had the courage to be vulnerable in front of others and a nation. It shares a message of how we can move beyond a very painful yesterday. In the words of Amanda, it is not to dissociate us from our right to be angry about the past, but by understanding that hatred will trigger more hatred into the future.

This truth came home after I recently watched a film about the Anglo-Boer war. A war where the acts of systemic genocide was committed by the British – then the most powerful nation in the world – against the most vulnerable people in the Boer Republics. Although I know no people who were involved, although I have faint memories of great-grandmothers sharing their stories about the aftermath of the Boer war, it is not something I have ever spent time thinking about. Yet, when the content of the film touched me, as a member of the Afrikaner community 125 years later, I experienced anger to the point of hatred, revulsion, and ironically, a need to get even. I shared this experience with Amanda, asking the big question: "Will we ever get to a point when some Black people will not be angry with the White people of this country?" Her answer was "highly unlikely!"

Her view highlighted the fact that nobody should be denied the right to their feelings. As a psychologist, I can identify with it. But her view went further and dealt with the issue of how not to let anger become hatred, because hatred not only destroys the fragile world of relationships, but also dehumanises the one who hates. Because hatred is such a powerful emotion, it absorbs attention, intent, and the freedom to act in ways that you choose. One should also own your choice on how you want to respond. It is a choice to experience the pain and anger from the past, but it is a conscious choice not to hate.

At the most humane level, Amanda's journey is one of a person whose past was shaped by emotional pain, never-ending hope of a better tomorrow, yet, a continuous frustration of that hope. It would have been OK for her to use it as a default position for giving up and checking out of life.

Instead, she chose not to. Instead, she chose to make her own decisions about how she wanted to respond. In her story and narrative, there is so much for all. In the book, she often veers off her journey in an attempt to contextualise and make sense to her readers, or perhaps, also to herself.

These more "academic" pieces not only provide interesting reading, but it also breaks the intensity of her narrative. What it does, however, brings a deeper insight into the book. Throughout the book, we are however challenged to rethink where we stand in relation to the content. This book lures the reader to rethink his/her response to the challenges we all encounter in our lives. It lingers in your mind, your heart and your soul.

Wessel Pretorius holds a BA (Hons) Psychology, MA (Counselling Psychology), MBA (University of Pretoria), MBA (exchange student) Rotterdam School of Business, CCC from the Oxford University (Said School of Business) and an Executive MSC in Business Studies from HEC (Paris).

He was also a founding Board member of the International Association of Change Management Professionals.

Foreword

They say you can tell how a person was raised by the character they exhibit in their lives. Honestly; in the world we live in today; it is very easy to see people, read their social media feed and fast make what we believe is an informed opinion of who they are.

I take such great pleasure in seeing people's reactions when I share my story with them. I come alive when I personally narrate where I have come from, what it has taken for me to get where I am, and the many things that are important to me.

It has been amazing to receive people's love and support as I journeyed through my life. I have found strength in the encouragement shown towards me by people who get to know me as I become more emotionally accessible. It took me a very long time to be able to do this. I had to work on myself and embrace the person before I could share who she truly is with the world.

I have been blessed with an incredible life, great family, friends, and a career that is a source of immense pride for me. But I did not just wake up and have all of that.

I have had to endure some incredible pain and hurt

in my life. I fought against all odds and pushed every boundary to prove that I was brought into this world for a purpose larger than my circumstances. I have had to fight off some of the most powerful demons and I continue to do so every day of my life because the horrors of my childhood will never stay at bay.

It is not possible to reduce my journey to just a few pages in a book, so this is by no means a full account of my life. This is a humble attempt at sharing with you some of the most defining moments and how I have managed to overcome some of life's toughest challenges, and come out on the other side, not only still standing but helping others in realising their own power within. As you will read throughout the book, I did not come out of these challenges unscathed; in fact, dealing with the impact is an everyday struggle.

This book is also not in any shape or form a platform to discredit or idolise the people whose actions have shaped my life. I myself have found comfort in the truth that wounds sustained in one's formative years never heal. Armed with knowledge, consciousness and information, as adults we find ways to shield or deal.

Early Life

I was born in 1978, in eSikhawini near eMpangeni, a township in northern KwaZulu Natal. The youngest of three, my father came from the Mthethwa, a very proud clan with a rich history as I grew to learn.

History tells us that the Mthethwa Empire was a Southern African state that arose in the 18th century south of Delagoa Bay and inland in eastern southern Africa. Mthethwa means "the one who rules".

History records further tell us that the Mthethwa people are part of the original Nguni category of a cluster of clans, whose modern identity dates back some seven hundred years. They are among the original Nguni groups who left the Great Lakes in Central Africa between 200 AD and 1200 AD.

On arrival in Southern Africa, they settled around modern-day Swaziland, mainly on the Lubombo Mountains, before leaving in the 17th century to settle in modern-day KwaZulu-Natal, in the Nkandla region. It consisted of roughly thirty Nguni Chiefdoms, lineages, and clans.

Unlike its successor, the Zulu Kingdom, the

Mthethwa Paramountcy was a confederation. After Zulu prince Sigidi kaSenzangakhona (better known as Shaka Zulu) became king, he forged a nearly homogeneous nation with a single king (Nkosi).

The Mthethwa Paramountcy was consolidated and extended under the rule of Dingiswayo. The chief entered into an alliance with the Tsonga to the north in the early 19th century and began trading ivory and other things with the Portuguese in Mozambique.

About 1811, the Buthelezi and a number of other Nguni groups, including the then still marginal Zulu clan led by Senzangakona, were integrated into a sort of confederacy with the Mthethwa clan predominating. Dingiswayo was killed in a battle with the Ndwandwe in 1817. The Mthethwa Paramountcy was superseded by the Zulu Kingdom under Shaka, a former lieutenant in the Mthethwa army.

Sadly, I never had the opportunity to sit around a fire with my father and listen to all these stories that ultimately led to the now majestic Zulu nation. I was barely a year old when he and my mother went their separate ways.

Rumor has it that my father was an abusive drunk who had multiple affairs in the neighborhood. He would apparently beat the living daylights out of my mother before storming out of the house to go sleep at one of his concubines across the road. Another rumor has it that they had high hopes that I would be the boy that would save my parents union – lo and behold, God had other plans. My mother still calls me "mfana" – the IsiZulu word meaning "young boy".

She used to tell me stories about how they were convinced that I was a boy and how I should have been a boy. My mother always pointed out – and still does – the many times I am supposedly acting like a boy. My eyes always violently roll up straight into my skull whenever she makes that reference. I always wondered why this conversation was the most topical thing in our very strained relationship.

She would tell me that, after the initial shock of giving birth to a girl they never wanted, she slowly started accepting her reality. My middle name is Siyaneliswa, meaning, "we are satisfied". However, things were not so satisfactory. My father wanted nothing to do with me. That was the end of them and promptly, the end of us.

My mother, a very beautiful Xhosa woman, took her offspring back to where she grew up; a very small village in a small town in the Transkei, called Mount Ayliff.

She was just twenty-six years old when she had me, a young lady with a world ahead of her.

At face value, you could say my childhood circumstances were no different from a lot of black children growing up in pre-1994 South Africa. We were not born free and we were confined to the demarcated areas for natives – the Bantustans or homelands, as they were known.

The Bantustans, established by the Apartheid Government, were areas to which the majority of the Black population was moved to prevent them from living in the urban areas of South Africa. They were a major administrative mechanism for the removal of Blacks from the South African political system under the many laws and policies created by Apartheid.

The idea was to separate Blacks from the Whites and give Blacks the responsibility of running their own independent governments, thus denying them protection and any remaining rights which a Black person could have in South Africa. In other words, Bantustans were established for the permanent removal of the Black population from White South Africa.

Segregation took place throughout the history of South Africa during the Apartheid era. SAHistory.org further says that segregation was defined as the imposed separation of groups; the practice of keeping ethnic, racial, religious, and gender groups separate.

The homelands started around the mid twentieth century, and ended in the late twentieth century, around the mid 1990s. The term that was used consistently was "White South Africa" as the Government aimed to move every Black person to his or her respective ethnic homeland in order to have South Africa completely in the hands of the White population. Blacks were given homelands, and that meant that whatever their culture was, they had to go to the given homeland.

For example, if a Black man or woman was of Zulu origin, they were assigned to go to KwaZulu, the Bantustan designated for Zulus. In total, ten homelands were created in South Africa. These were the Transkei, Bophuthatswana, Ciskei, Venda, Gazankulu, KaNgwane, KwaNdebele, KwaZulu, Lebowa, and QwaQwa.

The homelands were designed for specific ethnic groups. For example, the two homelands of Ciskei and Transkei were created only for the Xhosa people, while Bophuthatswana was created only for the Tswana people; KwaZulu was only for Zulu people, Lebowa for the Pedi and Northern Ndebele; Venda was only for Vendas; Gazankulu was for Tsonga people and Qwa Qwa was for Basothos.

The Apartheid government made it legal for Blacks to become citizens of their independent Bantustans. The Bantu Homelands Citizenship Act of 1970 was passed, which allowed Blacks living throughout South Africa to be legal citizens in the homeland designated for their particular ethnic group. The Act did not give Black people South African citizenship or civil and political rights. They had rights in their "Homelands", but they were not completely independent.

In the 1970s, the South African government declared four of the Bantustans "independent". These were the Transkei in 1976, Bophuthatswana in 1977, Venda in 1979, and Ciskei in 1981. The remaining Bantustans remained self-governing but had no independent rights.

Bantustans were to become independent from South Africa. This was a strategy to push all Black people out and have them isolated from South Africa. It meant that Black people would have to support themselves in these areas.

SAHistory.org says that the local homeland economies, however, were not developed. Bantustans relied almost entirely on White South Africa's economy. Farming was not very viable, largely because of the poor agricultural land in the homelands. In addition, Blacks owned only thirteen percent of South Africa's land. These farmlands were in poor condition because of soil erosion, and overgrazing. As a result, millions of Black people had to leave the Bantustans daily to work in the mines, on White-owned farms, for white families as domestic workers or gardeners, and for other industries in the cities. The homelands served as labour reservoirs, housing the unemployed and releasing them when their labour was needed in White South Africa.

Most of our parents were migrant labourers either in these mines, farms or in the suburbs as domestic workers.

The South African Homelands or Bantustans ceased to exist on 27 April 1994 and were re-incorporated into the new nine provinces of a democratic South Africa. These are Western Cape, Eastern Cape, Northern Cape, North West, Free State, Kwazulu Natal, Gauteng, Limpopo and Mpumalanga.

After separating from my father, my mother decided to leave her three young children with her extended family and set off for the City of Gold, Johannesburg in White South Africa to find work and better opportunities for herself.

My mother was an only child who lost both her parents when she was young. She remembers her father vaguely but has no recollection of her mother. Her paternal great-grandmother raised her as her paternal grandmother died when my mother was just six months old. She says she never had much connection to her maternal side except in recent years with her cousins.

She went off to Durban in KwaZulu Natal when she was just 15-years old to study. Well, life happened, and she ultimately met my father.

I am the last-born. Wait; read on, before you make all sorts of deductions about my life and how spoilt I must have been. Stay with me.

As a little girl, I longed for my mother's love and my father's protection. I had grown up being told – by the matriarch of the extended family and the aunts – that my mother had died. There was never any mention of my father. For a number of years, I lived with the fact that I did not have parents; I was an orphan.

The matriarch proceeded to change our last names from Mthethwa to her married last name early in our lives. She told the school and all the authorities that my mother was dead and that she was our official guardian. To be honest, I was never pre-occupied by my mother's death as I had no recollection of her. My reality was that I had no mother and no father.

As the years went by, I really struggled with a sense of identity, but my struggle was not about someone unilaterally changing my last name. Give me any other name and I will still be me. It was about the void of not having a real nurturing connection with a true mother figure. It was the lack of roots and no sense of who I was and where I had come from. I was just walking through life and growing up with no sense of direction, guidance, or acknowledgement.

I remember one day vividly. I must have been six or seven when a very beautiful lady showed up at our house. It was just past mid-noon and the sun was starting to mellow down. She was with my very kind aunt. I was too young to pay much attention, but I was captured by her beauty and found myself starring before I ran off.

I also grew up at a time when you had to disappear as a young kid when you saw an adult visitor. You had to be invisible, not to be seen nor heard. I was playing away feverishly outside when I was called to come in. It was the most defining moment of my life. It took a while before it sank in. For years, that day would haunt me. Honestly, it still does.

My aunt introduced the beautiful lady as my mother. The mother I was told was dead.

The manner in which adults handled things back then was just baffling and impolite. First, you have me believe that my mother is dead. For years you made be believe she was gone forever. My mind and my little heart had found a way to live without her, knowing she would never ever come back for me. Now, you introduce me to her! No epic explanation, nothing. It was a quick and very lame introduction. Did you forget that you told me she was dead? Could there have been a prelude to this horror movie?

I politely greeted her and went back outside to play as though nothing had happened. I was confused and honestly the moment was too big for my young mind to process, so it stored it away.

My sister's reaction was epic. She was two years older than I was and a little more aware of what was happening. She flat-out refused to acknowledge the woman as her mother. She told everyone the stories that we had been told – that our very kind aunt was "our mother". She protested at the news making headlines. None of us were ever the same again. My mother disappeared just as quickly as she was introduced to us.

The years after that epic event were confusing. I started processing everything.

At some point my little mind started thinking that she loved me and that is why she came back from the dead to be with me. My reality unfolded even more after that. She had vanished again. She may as well have stayed dead. I had found a way to live without her and just getting by. I felt even more alone than I had ever felt before.

I had started enduring a lot of abuse from the adults around who were meant to nurture and look after me. My one not-so-kind aunt would use every opportunity she had to tell me how useless I was. She used to tell me I would amount to nothing and that is why my mother did not want me. The adults who were remotely kind to me, unfortunately, did not live with us.

She would take the liberty of also telling my sister and I about how free our mother must have felt not having to look after us. She told us of the many men our mother was sleeping with and not even once thinking about us. All this animosity, because we ran across a floor she was mopping or stole scones she had baked. What were we supposed to do with this information?

I suffered severe abuse in my childhood. My self-esteem was under constant attack.

Havoca is an organisation run by survivors for adult survivors of child abuse. They provide support, friendship and advice for any adult whose life has been affected by childhood abuse. They write that your self-esteem is made up of personal beliefs and messages you received as a child that reflect how you value yourself. Self-esteem is either low or high, depending on the types of beliefs and messages.

They say that as an abused child, you develop a sense of low self-worth by replaying messages relayed to you by the abusive adults in your life. You also subtly incorporate some of these negative thoughts into your belief system.

Self-esteem is an important issue for everyone who was abused as a child. Your attempts to stop the abuse were most likely met with little or no success, which resulted in feelings of shame, helplessness, and incompetence. It is possible to carry these feelings with you into adult life and often they result in an individual's low self-esteem.

It is true that blaming yourself for the abuse is also very common. It is a manifestation of the low self-esteem. We do this because we were either overtly told by our abuser that it was our fault, or we are led to believe that it was our fault by covert messages we receive from others. Psychological abuse also attacks our self-esteem and forces it even lower. Name calling, put downs and insults all add up to give us the overall impression of low self-worth.

Having internalised these messages, we often play them back in our heads over and over again. As a result, we reinforce these negative feelings, which may result in depression, or destructive behaviours that serve only to further lower our self-esteem. They further say that negative self-talk is the act of putting yourself down through repeated negative thoughts. They play down your value as a human being and contribute to your feelings of depression, anger, or frustration. The messages come from our past, but they are spoken in our own voice, making them more believable.

In this book, I share the many ways I ensured that I did not internalise these negative messages. It is incredibly difficult to overcome and reverse the damage caused in your formative years. You will find in the chapters to come that there are severe consequences of long-term abuse. The impact on the victims can often be disastrous, and at times, lead to fatal outcomes.

Picking up the pieces

At a very early age, I needed a companion. I needed someone; something I knew would be my friend for life, no matter who else left me.

I turned to God for comfort. I became very active in the church. It was a church that my family never approved of, because it was too charismatic.

Early on in my life I had always gone to the traditional church with the matriarch. I always fell asleep or left to go play outside, earning myself the beating of a lifetime for that. So, I hated church, but had to find something to give me a sense of belonging.

I felt loved and comforted in the Lord. I was a cell leader as well as a praise and worship leader. I loved singing and nothing much has changed. I can sing.

For the first time in my life, I felt as though I belonged. I had something no one could take away no matter how hard they tried. I would be beaten up for coming home late because I was at church. Nothing deterred me. As you can tell I grew up in an era where beating was a way of life. It was tantamount to a talking to. It seems that the adults in our time knew no other way to communicate to a child. Oh, the ignorance and mis-education of our elders.

I was at home one Saturday morning when my spiritual teacher walked by my house. She called out for me and I went outside to talk to her. She looked at me with such disgust. I was very confused. My attire displeased her. I had shorts on and according to her; no child of God should dress in that manner. After lecturing me and quoting every single scripture in the bible, she dis-owned me and told me I had betrayed the church and all her teachings. As young as I was, I told her that we seem to have been serving different Gods because mine cares not about my clothes. I was shaking from shock and anger after this conversation. That was the end of that chapter and I felt so sad and alone but I was adamant her understanding of who God was did not align to mine. I no longer identified with her teachings as much as she felt I had betrayed them.

My mother was still nowhere to be seen. Life carried on. Frankly, her appearance – only to disappear again – caused way more harm. It was not fair, but I do not remember anyone ever making me a promise that life would be fair. This was my reality. I did not feel sorry for myself. In some way, she was still dead to me.

I kept myself busy. I always worked harder than most. At school, I was the youngest member of the school choir. I still sing the melodies we used to sing at school. Even this keeps bringing up so many mixed emotions.

Our music teacher used to shove board dusters in our mouths to make sure we opened them wide and round. Oh, how I remember the music tours we went on and the competitions we took part in as a very tight choir. It was a wonderful time when we boarded the bus to the University of Transkei for choir competitions. It was a much-needed and welcomed change of scenery. Both the church and the choirs gave me a sense of community and belonging.

I was also always the person who volunteered for everything at school. I loved smearing cow dung on the floor in our classroom. We were into eco-friendly ways of living long before it was fashionable. Of course, this was not considered fashion then; it was out of necessity. The cow dung kept the classroom cool in the summer heat and it looked amazing after I was done with it. This was a way of life in the rural communities.

I loved doing this because it had to be done after school. It was the only time I could be alone. I was not rushing home either, because of the vileness waiting for me. Above everything, it made me feel useful. It made me feel wanted, as I was doing something for others.

I also had a very keen interest in agriculture. I did not have a choice really. It was a mandatory subject, but I loved it so much. My plot always yielded the healthiest vegetables. I used to work on it after school and I would do anything to avoid going home. I still grow my own herbs and vegetables, a skill and passion I never lost.

My childhood was a mixed bag of simplicity, happiness, immeasurable pain, and confusion. My mother would pop back in every now and then to drop off some necessities, but she would not stay. I longed for her even more. It was torture seeing her, but never being able to access her, emotionally. We had no relationship. We were strangers to one another.

I would use the money she would leave for me to buy cold drinks and chips for the children at my school. I always felt I needed to share what I had with them. I would proudly tell them that my mother had brought it for me from Johannesburg. This was the only thing I could say about my mother and I just wanted them to know that there was someone who cared for me even if there were no signs of it.

Honestly, the money meant absolutely nothing to me. I felt disconnected from it. My relationship with money has probably never changed since then but I have grown to appreciate the value of it. I give it away as much as I can and use it to help those in need and change their lives for the better. I was also just in love with letting my teachers and the children know that I had a mother; but did I really?

I was very smart at school. For as long as I remember, I was always a top student, except for the time that boy Lulamile came to my school and challenged my position. For years after that, it was ping-pong between him and I.

I focused on my studies. A girl from my school became jealous of my achievements and started bullying me. Her name was Nolundi and I was terrified of her. She would randomly promise me a beating of a lifetime for no apparent reason. She would wait for me by the school gate when school was over. Her face was so terrifying. She was bigger than I was and did not have the most beautiful face. Perhaps it was the anger she was carrying that made her face the scariest I had ever seen. I will never know why she acted like that. I found a way to avoid her.

I would stay at school long after school was out. I would work on my plot.

One day, as I walking out of the pit toilets, I was captivated by a huge tree to my left. I soon learned that it was a Pearl Acacia. I found solace under that big tree. I would go and sit under this tree and start picking up the black seeds that it produced. They were the size of a granadilla seed and just as hard. That tree soon became my friend. It would produce stunning bright yellow flowers in the winter, and the seeds when it was done.

It became a symbol for me, as I started appreciating how seasons changed and that my season would come, too. It was just a matter of time. I would spend hours separating the seeds from the fine red soil.

Somehow, this was very therapeutic, and I would lose track of time. By the time the principal chased me away from the school, Nolundi had run out of steam and had gone home. I found ways to run away from her every time. As a result, she never got to me, but the mind games were enough to inject fear into my life. I felt debilitated. The stress was so intense that I developed sores all around my ankles, making it extremely difficult to walk. I would be so immobile at school whilst watching flies flock to my sores. It was a terrible time. It took a while but I soon healed.

Behind the hot coal stove

The family I grew up in had reasonable success. There were teachers, nurses, principals, and the matriarch had a general dealer shop. Another aunt owned a hardware store nearby. My very kind aunt who assumed the role of a mother figure for me, was studying to become a nurse. This meant she had to go and stay at the nursing school and someone had to look after her children and her husband and my sister had the first bite at the cherry.

I remember feeling so envious, because my uncle was a principal. They had lots of cars and they would go to town every weekend. They would go to Kokstad, where they would shop up a storm. That life just seemed so appealing. The little ones were also just so adorable.

My sister did not stay for long, though. My uncle was physically abusive and she just could not take it, so I was given the chance. In fact, I volunteered to go look after their children, cook for him, and wash his clothes. I had not even turned ten as yet, but it was an amazing opportunity to be useful.

I had to get away from the house I lived in. It was unbearable.

See, I had another uncle who had decided that I was woman enough to fulfill his sexual desires. He would gather a few of the young children and play music for all of us in the secluded formal lounge. He would proceed to lift me up and pretend to be dancing with me, but he was hurting me.

I had no one to talk to. I had no one to protect me. I hoped my sister and the other children could see what was happening, but no one ever said anything. He told me he would expel me from the house if I told anyone. He said no one would believe me anyway.

I also felt that it was my fault. My cruel aunts would always tell me, during their tirades against me that I had legs that would attract men, like my mother did. I guess the shape of my legs gave my uncle the right to violate me.

I felt guilty and ashamed. I could have easily started hating my body and myself, but I refused to give in. I was determined to rise above it all. I had a plan to be free, but I just needed to be patient, and make it through the other side. I believed that one day, the seasons would change and I would be free.

Susanne Babbel Ph.D., M.F.T. writes that there are various types of traumatic events that can lead to Post Traumatic Stress Disorder (PTSD). She explains that sexual abuse is a particularly sinister type of trauma, because of the shame it instills in the victim. With childhood sexual abuse, victims are often too young to know how to express what is happening and seek out help. When not properly treated, this can result in a lifetime of PTSD, depression and anxiety.

The trauma that results from sexual abuse is a syndrome that affects not just the victim and their family, but all of our society. Because sexual abuse, molestation, and rape are such shame-filled concepts, our culture tends to suppress information about them.

According to childtrauma.org, one out of three females and one out of five males in the U.S. have been victims of sexual abuse before the age of eighteen years. And according to the American Academy of Experts in Traumatic Stress (AAETS), 30% of all male children are molested in some way, compared to 40% of females. Some of the most startling statistics unearthed during research into sexual abuse are that children are three times as likely to become victims of rape than adults, and stranger abuse constitutes by far the minority of cases. It is more likely for a child to experience sexual abuse at the hands of a family member or another supposedly trustworthy adult. It affects children and adults across ethnic, socioeconomic, educational, religious, and regional lines.

I jumped at the opportunity to go live with my other uncle and his kids just below the matriarch's household. I wanted to get away from my evil aunts and my sexually abusive uncle, but I was still not far enough.

Looking after the young girls was my escape. My very kind aunt would come by every two to three weeks or so and we would cook and bake. It was such a special time with her. She filled a gap, if only momentarily. She was very kind and I thank God for her everyday. She showed me love; my only wish was that she could stay for longer, but she had to go back to nursing school.

This life soon lost its shine because of the physical abuse. I was literally a punching bag, as was my aunt and the kids. I got it the most, because I was the next thing to an adult in the house.

If the lights were not on at a certain time, I would be punched in the face. I really wanted to leave, but I had nowhere else to go. It was the better of the worse evils. I stayed and just hung in there. I knew my day for liberation would come; I just did not know how or when. I just had to brave through it all.

A little part of me hoped my mother would come and rescue me, because I wrote her a letter once and told her what had been happening to me. I was not sure if she received it, because nothing ever came of it. I wrote many after that; the outcome was always the same – nothing.

One day, there was commotion in the matriarch's homestead. It turns out my pedophile uncle had been involved in a car accident. The van he was driving just veered off the bridge and capsized without any other car involved. He was with my brother and his friend. They both walked away without a scratch.

My uncle, on the other hand, was not in good shape. I froze and went into shock when I heard he had been hospitalised. I later learnt he would be paralysed "for life". He lost his speech and all mobility.

I broke down and I bawled my eyes out. No one took notice of course, because I was always so invisible. My reaction was for completely different reasons to everyone's.

That was the day he no longer had power over me. That was the day God saved me from what seemed to be a lifetime of shame, violation, molestation, and stripping of my dignity. I felt free, for the first time in my life; my seasons were changing.

I continued staying at my other uncle's house. The physical abuse was a way of life. It was an everyday thing for me. It reached a point at which I ran away one day and went to hide at the matriarch's house.

He came after me and I could not escape fast enough. My only option was hiding behind a piping hot coal stove. The matriarch tried to distract him. She was his mother, but there were days when even she could not tame him. I stood behind that stove for what seemed like a lifetime.

I opted to roast there rather than come out and face

the beatings; and did I roast? My eyes were blood-shot, and looked as though they were about to pop out by the time his mother managed to distract him away from the kitchen. He was in beastly mode that night, and I was afraid he was going to kill me. If it was my day to die, I was happy to roast to death instead.

Our home was powered by a generator. Every night, someone had to suck the petrol out of the car to fuel up the generator. This wonderful chore was specifically reserved for me, of course.

One day, I was busy sucking the petrol out of his Cressida when I received the biggest slap of my life across my eyes. I blacked out and fell to the ground. The petrol oozed all over me. I can still smell it every time I relate the incident.

He was a heavy smoker, too, and that day could have ended very badly for all of us, had he just dropped his cigarette. I received no explanation for the beating.

I was later told that someone saw me in the vicinity of boys who were teasing the dogs at the matriarch's house. She had a shop that she had rented out to a white gentleman. He had big dogs and the boys loved teasing them and then running away. My sin on that day was to be in the vicinity. The fact that our house was right below the matriarch's house and I went pass there every day after school, did not matter. I had no voice. I had no right to speak or explain.

Out of all the moments I had suffered physical,

emotional, and sexual abuse this was the most difficult for me. I arrived at school the next day, and my friend told me she saw what happened as she was walking past our yard. She was in such shock because of what she saw. I felt so ashamed and embarrassed. It was also sadly the day I lost her, because she just distanced herself from me from that day onwards. I did not get it then, and I still do not get it now, but I have made sense of it.

That uncle sadly died at the tender age of forty-nine from liver cirrhosis living behind a wife and two young girls.

What are the odds?

The Australian Institute of Family Studies says that child abuse and neglect refers to any behaviour by parents, caregivers, other adults, or older adolescents that is outside the norms of conduct and entails a substantial risk of causing physical or emotional harm to a child or young person. Such behaviours may be intentional or unintentional and can include acts of omission (i.e., neglect) and commission (i.e., abuse) (Bromfield, 2005; Christoffel et al., 1992; Gilbert et al., 2009). The five main subtypes of child abuse and neglect are physical abuse, emotional maltreatment, neglect, sexual abuse and witnessing family violence. I experienced all of them.

The consequences of experiencing child abuse and neglect will vary considerably. For some adults, the effects of child abuse and neglect are chronic and debilitating; other adults have less adverse outcomes, despite their histories (Miller-Perrin & Perrin, 2007). Critical factors that may influence the way child abuse and neglect affects adults include the frequency and duration of maltreatment and if more than one type of maltreatment has occurred.

Chronic maltreatment is defined as "recurrent incidents of maltreatment over a prolonged period of time" (Bromfield & Higgins, 2005, p. 39) has been linked to worse outcomes than transitory or isolated incidents of maltreatment (e.g., Ethier, Lemelin, & Lacharite, 2004; Graham et al., 2010; Johnson-Reid, Kohl, & Drake, 2012).

The Australian Institute of Family Studies' research suggests that maltreatment types are interrelated; that is, a large proportion of adults who experience childhood abuse or neglect are exposed to more than one type of abuse (known as multi-type maltreatment). Further to this, other forms of victimisation (known as poly-victimisation) such as bullying or assault by a peer have often been found to co-occur with child maltreatment (Finkelhor, Ormrod, & Turner, 2007). Their research indicates that those who experience multi-type maltreatment and/or poly-victimisation are more likely to experience high levels of trauma symptoms and worse outcomes as adults than those who are exposed to no maltreatment or only one type (Finkelhor et al., 2007; Higgins & McCabe, 2001; Richmond, Elliot, Pierce, Aspelmeier, & Alexander, 2009).

In attempting to explain some of the adverse outcomes associated with chronic and multi-type maltreatment a concept that is often employed is complex trauma. Complex trauma reflects the multiple and interacting symptoms, disorders and multiple adverse experiences and the broad range of cognitive, affective, and behavioural outcomes associated with prolonged trauma, particularly if occurring early in life and involving an interpersonal element (e.g., sexual abuse; Price-Robertson, Rush, Wall, & Higgins, 2013).

In her article *Survivors of Abuse*, Sharie Steins says that abuse in any form or context can harm an individual. Even after the abuse has stopped, survivors can still experience distress. Abuse survivors have a higher risk of mental health concerns. They may experience one or more of the following issues:

- Anxiety: Survivors may be afraid of people or situations that remind them of their abuse experiences. They may be fearful of strangers, solitude, or sexual intimacy, depending on the nature of the abuse. Anxiety symptoms such as disrupted sleep or panic attacks are common in survivors of abuse.

- Anger: Survivors of abuse may feel intense anger at their abusers. They may resent bystanders who knew of the abuse and failed to intervene. They might even be mad at themselves for being abused, believing they could or should have stopped it. Anger is a natural response to being abused. Survivors can learn to manage their anger in a constructive manner that will promote healing.

- Depression: Feelings of sadness or emptiness are common among people who have experienced abuse. They may struggle to enjoy activities they used to like, especially if those activities remind them of the abuser.

- Dissociation: Numbness, confusion, and out-of-body experiences may occur during or after abuse. Dissociation can help the person avoid the pain and fear associated with abuse. In rare cases, memories of abuse may be repressed. Some survivors may not have any conscious memory of the abuse.

- Mood issues: Irritability and mood swings affect many survivors of abuse.

- Post-traumatic Stress (PTSD): Nightmares, hyper vigilance, flashbacks, and other symptoms of PTSD may occur. Survivors are likely to avoid certain settings and situations that remind them of the abuse.

- Shame: Survivors often experience guilt and shame. They may believe they deserved the abuse, were responsible for it, or failed to stop it. Challenging these beliefs in therapy can help survivors of abuse transform these feelings.

- Self-Destructive Behavior: Self-destructive behavior can take many forms. Some survivors will self-medicate with drugs or alcohol. Others might engage in self-harm, such as burning or cutting themselves. People may neglect their personal hygiene or sabotage any potential for success. These behaviors often indicate low self-esteem.

- Trust Issues: Learning to trust others after abuse has occurred can be challenging. Someone who has experienced abuse may struggle with physical intimacy.

While abuse can lead to mental health concerns, not every case results in extreme distress. The severity of the consequences depends on the situation. For instance, someone may feel differently about abuse from a parent and abuse from a stranger. Whether loved ones choose to recognise or dismiss the abuse can have a large impact.

Demographic factors can also affect how someone responds to abuse. For example, someone who experiences abuse during childhood is more likely to develop mental health concerns. Gender roles can influence how one responds to sexual abuse. Socioeconomic status may decide whether someone receives adequate treatment.

Other factors that may affect the consequences of child abuse and neglect on adult survivors include:

- the age and developmental stage at which maltreatment occurred: some evidence suggests that the younger the child was at the time of the onset of the maltreatment, the more likely they are to experience problems later in life;

- the severity of maltreatment: the greater the severity of abuse or neglect, the higher the likelihood of negative outcomes;

- the type/s of abuse and/or neglect: different sub-types of maltreatment may be related to different negative outcomes;

- the victim/survivor's perceptions of the abuse: worse outcomes are likely if there are feelings of self-blame, shame or stigmatisation;

- the relationship the victim/survivor had (or has) with the perpetrator: for example, in child sexual abuse increased negative affects tend to be associated with the perpetrator being a father, father-figure or someone with whom the child has an intense, emotional relationship;

- whether the abuse or neglect was detected and action taken to assure the safety of the child (e.g., child protection intervention);

- positive or protective factors that may have mitigated the effects of maltreatment (e.g., family support, perpetrator readiness for change); and

- whether victims/survivors received therapeutic services to assist them in recovery (Bromfield & Higgins, 2005; Miller-Perrin & Perrin, 2007;

Price-Robertson et al., 2013).

Adverse outcomes of abuse and neglect often emerge in childhood and adolescence and may continue in adults with histories of abuse and neglect (Miller-Perrin & Perrin, 2007).

Some evidence suggests that adults who were abused or neglected as children are at increased risk of intergenerational abuse or neglect compared to those who were not maltreated as children (Kwong, Bartholomew, Henderson, & Trinke, 2003; Mouzos & Makkai, 2004; Pears & Capaldi, 2001).

In a study by Pears and Capaldi (2001), parents who had experienced physical abuse in childhood were significantly more likely to engage in abusive behaviours toward their own children or children in their care. Oliver (1993), in a review of the research literature, concluded that an estimated one-third of children who are subjected to child abuse and neglect go on to repeat patterns of abusive parenting towards their own children. Although this is a significant number, it is also important to note that Oliver's estimations indicate that a majority of maltreated children do not go on to maltreat their own children.

Kwong and colleagues (2003) determined that growing up in abusive family environments can teach children that the use of violence and aggression is a viable means for dealing with interpersonal conflict, which can increase the likelihood that the cycle of violence will continue when they reach adulthood. I have very strong opinions on this matter and I will be discussing it a little bit later when I refer to the nature vs. nurture debate and free will.

Research suggests that adults, particularly women, who were victimised as children are at risk of re-victimisation in later life (Cannon, Bonomi, Anderson, Rivara, & Thompson 2010; Mouzos & Makkai, 2004; Whiting, Simmons, Havens, Smith, & Oka, 2009; Widom, Czaja, & Dutton, 2008).

The Australian Institute of Family Studies further says that findings from the Australian component of the International Violence Against Women Survey (IVAWS) indicated that 72% of women who experienced either physical or sexual abuse as a child also experienced violence in adulthood, compared to 43% of women who did not experience childhood abuse (Mouzos & Makkai, 2004). Further to this, a review of approximately ninety sexual victimisation studies found that over thirty studies had reported a link between child sexual assault and sexual re-victimisation in adulthood (Classen, Gronskaya Palesh, & Aggarwal, 2005).

In a prospective study by Widom and colleagues (2008), all types of childhood victimisation (physical abuse, sexual abuse and neglect) measured were associated with increased risk of lifetime re-victimisation. Findings indicated that childhood victimisation increased the risk for physical and sexual assault/abuse, kidnapping/stalking, and having a family friend murdered or commit suicide (Widom et al., 2008). Women who experience childhood violence or who have witnessed parental violence could be at risk of being victimised as adults as they are more likely to have low self-esteem and they may have learnt that violent behaviour is a normal response to dealing with conflict (Mouzos & Makkai, 2004).

Clearly the odds for victims of abuse are stacked against them with very slim chances of ever breaking the cycle. But is it that dire? What about the ability to choose? I understand and appreciate the facts. They are what they are but could maltreated people decide that they know what that life is like and that they want better for themselves and their children?

Holding out for a change

Silently, I knew that my life would one-day change for the better. No, I did not think that my mother would be the one to come and save me. It seemed as though that ship had sailed a long time ago. My father never even crossed my mind. He was nowhere to be seen; he had never come for me. I had no introduction to him or his family. He was like a ghost.

I just had this undying belief that one day, I would be older and I could be responsible for my own life. I decided that I was not going to be one of the statistics that did not make it out on the other side. I wanted to beat the odds.

It seemed big people were doing whatever they wanted to do, so I looked forward to the day I became a big person. Only, I had no intention of inflicting so much pain on another, especially children. I knew what pain felt like. I wanted to stop that from happening. I wanted to stand up and speak for those who think they have no voice. I wanted to give people a chance at a dignified life. I had to be successful so that I could be an example to many people out there. I wanted to let people know that you can be whatever you want to be but I needed to have achieved significant success for my story to have impact. I knew that from a very early age. I also knew that I had to be patient and wait out my years.

I needed something to keep me going. My spirituality and my belief in God's love were all that ever kept me sane. I always wanted to be in the presence of the Lord. I always wanted to praise him, tears streaming down my face. I never lost my faith in him.

At no point in my life did I ever despise God or question why my life was so painful. At no point did I wish I had not been born. I had this deep-seated feeling that there was a greater purpose for me. I never deeply internalised any of the abuse. I never believed that I would amount to nothing. I refused to believe that the God who brought me here would want to see me fail.

It was very difficult to hear the negative words and doom scripts, but I had cemented it in my mind that it was not true. So, I made sure none of it stuck. It hurt like hell, but I refused to let my mind believe it. Life carried on and so did my chores.

I would sing out loud as I ran through the cornfields fetching mealies to roast on the fire. I was always the one fetching the mealies. I had to stay relevant. I had to be needed for something.

I can still feel the raindrops against my little body as I ran through the field quickly picking the mealies and running back, because I was afraid of thunder and lightning. Every summer afternoon was characterised by heavy storms, but someone had to go out there and bring home the bacon – or the mealies, as it were.

Children process pain in whatever way seems appropriate for them. One day, I just woke up and stopped wearing shoes. I would go to school with my full uniform, gym dress pressed to perfection, but no shoes. I used to have frostbite. This carried on for weeks until my heels had started cracking badly. Snow was a common thing in my village, but I refused to wear shoes.

It was a very big issue that led to endless school interventions but I refused to wear them. Then, one day I woke up and put shoes on again. I could hear a collective sigh of relief. I cannot explain what was going on there but I can assure you I have made up for lost time. I cannot walk barefoot at all, even in the house. I cannot stand the feeling I experience when my feet touch grass. No beach sand, no grass, please.

Maybe this time

One rare occasion, my mother sent for us to come visit her in Johannesburg. It was nice of her. She lived in a squatter camp, Mshenguville, not far from Kliptown in Soweto. Mshenguville was one of the designated informal settlements for the migrant labourers who had come to White South Africa to seek work. Often, those who were fortunate enough to have found work, would have to support those who had not found work. It was a real community. It was a shock to my system but I cared more about being with her. I would have slept under the bridge if it meant I could be with her.

I was so scared of her. It was the strangest feeling of happiness mixed with terror. We were strangers and had probably grown even more apart over the years since she showed up from the dead.

I remember seeing the Johannesburg lights as we left Heidelberg. Those lights still get me every time. They represented so much hope. It just felt as if she would finally tell us to stay. She never did, of course; it was just a pipe dream.

At the time, we still needed passports to come to

Johannesburg as South Africa was not accessible to the Bantus. I was too young to have one, so I would be smuggled in. I had to hide under the seat in the minibus until we went past the border post at Bulwer and Montrose, where police would most likely stop the minibus.

This was my birth country, and I was not free. Heartache came in so many different forms.

A lot of things made no sense. I did not care, though; I just wanted to be with my mother. I was so scared of her, but longed for her. It is the loneliest feeling ever. She was there, but she was so far removed from me. She was a stranger. Our visits would not be very long, and the minibus would soon fetch us to take us back home. I do remember often wondering if I would ever see her again.

You might be wondering what ever happened to my father. Well, he never came back for us. I have never met him after I was born and I guess even that can be debated.

I do not know what it is like to have a father. My mother was not forthcoming in giving any information or facilitating any kind of introduction. She kept saying she did not know where he was. It was as though he never existed. I feel immensely robbed of this part of my life, but I had to let it go.

There was that time when I made myself a promise that once I started working, I would hire a private investigator to find him. It would cost me ten thousand rand, but I was going to save up for it and find him. Once I had the money, I just started wondering why I wanted to find someone who should have been moving mountains to find me, but never bothered. What did I need him for, now that I was older? I may have needed him the most when I was younger, but he opted out; he wanted nothing to do with me, so why bother imposing myself on someone who wished I had not been born? The sadness of it all is that he was never there to give me his side of the story. So, how could I know for sure?

I admire people who have come from backgrounds where they had the nurturing of one parent or both. I could not identify with this, but it never stopped me from believing and understanding that because I did not have that, does not make me any less of a human being.

I am like a fish out of water when people go on and on about their parents and the sacrifices they made for them. It is amazing, but I have absolutely no connection to it, except a reminder of how I never had that. It does not stop me from admiring it and telling them to appreciate it, because not everyone has experienced it. I am a mother now and that has been the greatest lesson of love for me. I now know what those parents gave to these people and why they are so proud of them. I live every moment of my life making sure that I am the one my children and those in my care talk about with great admiration and fondness. This is not for them to idolise or adore me but to have experienced their right to love and nurture.

That is it! We are done.

Being told that my father and my mother wanted nothing to do with my siblings or me was a way of life. The irony is, even if I wanted to dispute these claims, I could not. My mother and father were not there. They had indeed abandoned us and there was truth to these claims. So, how could I not believe them when they told me I would amount to nothing?

I had a roof over my head, food, and clothes on my back, but it felt like the price for all of that was too high. We enjoyed some of the conveniences of modern life. We grew our own fruits and vegetables. We had our own livestock, goats, sheep, cattle, pigs, and chickens.

Some of my chores included collecting fresh eggs every morning and cleaning the chicken coup. I learnt how to milk cows as well. It was also my duty to feed the pigs every morning and afternoon. The matriarch's shop was a pension pay point for our village.

The most intense days were the ones leading up to pension payout. I would have to give the pigs extra feed for them to grow twice as fast with the sole aim of getting maximum fat from them. The pigs would get slaughtered the day before the pension payday. I can still hear the screams of those pigs. They haunt me every time I see bacon or a pork chop.

They would run away as though they knew what awaited them. The raw layers of pig fat and oil drained from cooked pork were a best seller on pension days. It was believed that the oil kept the evil spirits away. I would have you know that my stomach cannot handle pork until this day. The best I can do is bacon but even that must be crispy and all I can see are those pigs every time I take a bite into the crunch.

The matriarch also taught us how to make candles. I have so many fond memories of the simple life. We were very self-sufficient, and this is something I have carried throughout my life. Unfortunately, it also came with the abuse, which created an enormous amount of confusion and inner conflict.

I did not long for much, except the safety and love of my parents. I longed for that sense of belonging, a place I could call home. It was time we tried to obtain it.

In 1991, when I was thirteen years old, my brother, sister and I hatched a plan to run away. We had remembered the minibus that took us to our mother and kept tracking it when it went past the bus stop. It would go to Johannesburg every Sunday afternoon.

One sunny Sunday, we shoved a few of our belongings in one bag and ran away. We literally ran away. We skipped the fence, did not say good-bye to anybody, and ran for our lives. We never looked back. We kept running.

We had no money and had carried that one bag. We reached the bus stop, seemingly undetected, as we nervously waited for the minibus. We kept hoping no one would notice we were gone. It seemed no one did. The minibus came after what felt like a life-time of waiting hiding behind the trees and off we went. That was it!

That was the end of a brutal chapter and we had no idea what awaited us on the other side, but we were very happy to take that risk. We wanted to get to know another devil because the one we knew all those years was no longer serving us. In fact, it never served us in the way we hoped for.

It was four o'clock in the morning when we knocked on my mother's door, unannounced.

We had made it through the brutal police at the South African border post, Bulwer. I still had to hide underneath the seat and this time, I had to stare at the tarmac underneath as the minibus had holes on the floor patched with disintegrating, old carpet. The heat from the engine was too much to bear, but I had to. I was no stranger to situations like that.

I felt that this was the last and only chance to be with my mother; there was no looking back.

She was 40-years old. She had a new husband, and there we were; three teenagers gasping for the love of their mother. To be honest, I am romanticising this; we just wanted to remind her that we exist.

The abuse I suffered was not only reserved for me. My brother and my sister also had their fair share of hardship. We had reached a boiling point, we simply could not carry on living the way we did. We had to break free. Ironically, it was just a year after Nelson Mandela was released from twenty-seven years of prison for fighting for Black people's rights. White South Africa was on fire, literally.

Where to from here?

It was a really difficult time for all concerned. My brother was eighteen, my sister fifteen and I, just thirteen years old.

We tried our best to assimilate into the life in Johannesburg. It was a very strange time, as we would find ourselves running from teargas and burning tires on the streets. People were being killed and there were curfews. The country was burning.

Soweto was very new and scary for me. It was overwhelming, but I just enjoyed running through the little alleys in-between the shacks as we went to buy chicken feet or ice-lollies.

There was so much culture and character, but it was a dangerous place. We lived in a time when gangsters were at their prime as well. Young, fresh girls like us were ripe for the picking. Kidnappings were an everyday thing; everyone was on the edge and no one was safe. Girls would be taken, raped and often killed.

It was terrifying, and as such, we always had to stay close to home. Some were daring and would snatch you right under your family's nose. The pit toilets were a long walk away from our shacks, and this was always an opportunity to be grabbed, so we had to have a clearly thought out plan for our humanely needs.

In the night, we used a potty. Like little babies, we used potties to do our business right in the middle of the living area in our shacks, and we had to clear it in the mornings. This was the everyday life of Black people in White South Africa. It was natural to think of the life I had back in the Transkei; a life of seeming luxury, but nothing could take me back there. This was the devil I was willing to get to know and live with.

We were soon moved to a housing project in Orange Farm, south of Johannesburg. I remember the protests that ensued when people were informed they would be moved. I did not understand why people would kick against being given houses and would rather live in inhumane conditions like Mshenguville, in shacks.

But, their lives were there – these communities were built and bonded by tough times. They had raised children there. I still did not get it. I have never seen such despicable conditions. It was a shame, an injustice, and a legacy of apartheid that stripped our people of their dignity.

We moved to Orange Farm. It was far south of Johannesburg. The houses were still being built, and ours was not yet complete, so we had to build and live in another shack. At least now, there was hope. We were in our own little plot of land and our own house was taking shape right in front of our eyes. We always slept on the floor in the living area of the shack, as there was only one bedroom for my mother and her husband. Life carried on. It also felt like we could finally be free and shielded from a parallel that was going on, the supposed tribal war between the Xhosas and the Zulus. This was and remains a very complicated part of our recent history. I will not do justice to it, suffice to say, thousands of people lost their lives purely because of the tribe they were. We would visit my mother's relative in the East Rand township of Vosloorus and we would have to run for our lives from machete and gun-wielding men. It was frightening.

Education. What education?

I went to an Indian school in Lenasia South, Johannes-burg, which was about fifteen kilometers away. I was lost. The standard of education was unlike our Bantu education. It was tough to grasp the concepts in the time required.

The workload was overwhelming. I was doing fifteen subjects. I was like a fish out of water. I just did not fit in, and could not cope, but I kept at it. This was just another hurdle I had to overcome.

I would catch the early morning train from Orange Farm to the Lawley station, and still had another four kilometers to walk to school through grass as tall as I was. It was terrifying. I felt as though I was still not free. Some days, I would cry all the way to the school, and just kept looking over my shoulder. I did not feel safe. I was, however, willing to make a go for it.

That very year, my mother decided to send me to Lesotho. I did not understand that at all, as I was starting to get a hang of it. I was failing some subjects, but I was gaining some momentum. I felt she was really just trying to get rid of me again. Off I went to a country where they spoke a language I had never spoken before. I was a rural Xhosa girl, thrown straight in the deep end all over again. As expected, the school in Lesotho did not admit me, because I did not speak SeSotho as a first language. Go figure.

My mother had a friend who worked at the school and hence, she thought this was a brilliant idea. The school was indeed a great school, renowned for excellence. It was just not the right school for me. I thought my mother would take the opportunity to connect with me somehow, but there she was, shipping me off again; abandoning me, and letting me rot in a foreign country. What was she expecting of me? She did not even come with me. Again, this was just another obstacle in my way.

I was told to learn to speak, read, and write Sesotho before they could consider me.

I went to live with my mother's friend's mother in the mountains of Lesotho in a place called Tshosang, outside Maseru. She was blind and lived in a little hut. My job was to look after her whilst I learnt the language.

It was just the two of us. The days were long, dark, cold, and empty, but I kept my head down. I read Sesotho books. The old lady spoke no other language, so I was forced to learn very quickly. I still feel emotional when I tell people about my time in Lesotho.

One day, I caught a bus to go buy some supplies from town. I remember thinking and wishing that my mother could just grow a conscious and come fetch me. I did not understand what I was doing there after the rejection from the school. I grew to appreciate that she thought this was best for me. Sadly, I had no trust in any of her decisions by this time and I felt that she was just getting rid of me all over again. I had just found her and all I wanted was to give our relationship a chance. I just wanted her to be my mother.

I was thirsty for her love and affection, but I had taught myself not to be needy. This, for me, was just another episode in my journey. I told myself to just buckle down and wait out my years, but I was baking in the pain.

I thought I had started to hallucinate when I heard my mother's voice. I turned and looked through the crowd, waiting to board the mini bus back to Tshosang.

But there she was. Words will never describe how I felt that very moment. I was cautiously happy to see her and overwhelmed with relief. She was a familiar face in a very foreign place for me, even as foreign as we were to one another. We went back home the very next day.

I had lost a year through the upping and downing in different schools. I needed to find a way to pass that year, otherwise it would have been a waste. I refused to give up. I went to one of the schools in the township and asked to just sit for the exam. The principal at the first school I tried, declined my request. I was disappointed but kept trying. The next one told me I was mad, but he would let me write. I ended up topping the class.

I enrolled at what seemed like a *fly by night* private school in the middle of town in 1993 to do standard nine (grade eleven). I felt crushed when I was sent back to do my standard eight because I was too young. It was so disappointing after all that I had been through but the school was not negotiating.

I did not appreciate the schooling system in Johannesburg. In the Transkei, it did not matter; if you passed you went to the next grade. My cousin completed her matric at the age of fifteen; it was common. Anyway, I had to oblige, because I needed stability in my life. However, this was another setback.

I lived with my mother for the next couple of years while I was in high school. It was tough. She struggled to make ends meet. She worked as an orthodontic nurse, but never had so many mouths to feed before.

Her husband worked in the mines but did not really earn much. There were days when we went to school with no money for lunch. Friends shared some of their food with me on those days.

I found solace, peace and escape in my books. My days started very early in the morning. I would catch the five-thirty train to the city and walk to school. I was in a girl's school and I was really enjoying it. My sister and her friend were in the same school so I felt comfortable.

I recall the year 1994, when there was just real chaos across the country. This was the year of the first democratic elections in South Africa. One day, there was heavy violence in town and to be safe, the school sent all of us home very early, but my train back home was only at three o'clock.

My friend, Winnie, lived in town, so we decided to walk to her mother's flat. We were hungry, so we walked to stores in nearby Hillbrow to buy some food. We were walking through parked minibus taxis.

One moment, Winnie was walking in front and the next second, she took a very sharp turn and ran away from some guy who was approaching. I remember the guy bumping me and then swearing at me for being in his way.

I found that strange, but before I could take a few more steps, I felt a sharp pain in my spine. I felt dizzy and I asked my friends to wait for me as I sat down. I instinctively touched my spine and there was a hole through my blazer. My hand came back smeared in the blood that was oozing out of my back.

He had stabbed me. I did nothing to him. I did not know him, but he just stabbed me. And just like that, he had disappeared.

I was terrified to tell my mother that I had been stabbed in the middle of town, because she would have asked what I was doing there to begin with.

Anyway, we went to a nearby clinic, and fourteen stitches later I was discharged. The clinic had insisted on calling my mother and tell her what had happened. To say she was less than impressed is an understatement. This was also just a serious inconvenience for her. I love Johannesburg so much, but I can assure you my initial introduction to it was brutal.

I never gave my mother any trouble, except the time when I developed a gambling problem. I would return from school and go to play card games with some kids from the township. I was trying to fit in.

One day, the game would just not end, and there must have been five rand at stake – enough to buy me lunch at school the next day. She got back from work and I was not there and had not cooked supper.

I had lost track of time. I had no idea where my siblings were. She was so upset; she threw every piece of vegetable in the house at me. It took a while for me to break free from that gambling addiction, but I learnt to go home when it was time for homework and chores. I never wanted another tomato or onion lending on my face again. I just did not enjoy letting her down.

She always had her hands full with my brother and sister. I felt lonely most of the time, but this was no different to the feeling I had all those years growing up without her. Perhaps then it was bearable because she was not there. This time, she was there, but I did not know her, and neither did she know me.

I buried myself in my books. I excelled at school just as I did all those years back in the Transkei. I was getting my mojo back all over again.

You could really say that a person's character is largely shaped by their upbringing. Things that we experience in our formative years play a significant role in who we become.

In the book *When you and your mother can't be friends,* Victoria Secunda says, "…we forget in order to survive our childhoods, when we are totally dependent on our parent's goodwill; but to recover from such childhoods, we must begin by remembering the bad and the good". She continues to say, "We must allow the feelings of loss to surface rather than be unconsciously rerouted and bubble up in other relationships".

My earliest relationship in high school was with a guy twelve years my senior. It was only after three years in that relationship that I realised that I was just trying to find my father in him.

The relationship was toxic. He was a serial cheat, but would buy me off with expensive gifts and lunches. I ended it on the day I started my university life. I needed a clean slate, a new beginning. I knew I deserved better.

I still did not do very well with relationships for a long time. I met great people, but I left long before they could have a chance to leave me. I ran away every time a relationship started becoming too intense or serious.

I had to work on myself. I had no business hurting other people, so I laid off relationships for a while.

Whilst kissing the frogs, I also had an encounter with an abusive one. Having grown up under extreme abuse, I could see the signs. I warned him multiple times to not ever touch me and that he would regret it. He, of course, could not help himself.

One day he manhandled me very badly and pinned me down on the bed and was shaking me hard, trying to beat me up. That was a big mistake on his part.

I defended myself. I kicked him very hard in his sensitive parts and I fought him off with everything I had. I managed to break free and ran out. That was the end of the fling. No one was ever going to treat me that way, ever again, so I decided he was not worth it.

A beckoning dream

My mother really struggled to make ends meet, but this never bothered me that much. I made do with the little we had. I was with her and maybe that was all I needed, even though we still had no relationship; it was strange living with her.

I am also not sure what I expected from her, from us. There was not real effort at the time to build the relationship. To tell the truth, I have always been in a shell-shocked state with my mother.

She had a friend that she worked with, who had a daughter my sister's age. She would give us clothes that her daughter no longer wore. It was the only reason we could even have clothes on our back.

I was most frustrated at school when it was civvies day. I had nothing to wear but she would save me. I do this for people now, because I know what a big difference it makes. She helped to give me some dignity. I am forever grateful to her and her daughter for their kindness.

I was preparing to write my matric exams when I was told I would not be able to do so without a South

African identity document. I had never needed one before.

This was a serious issue. I had no birth certificate and nowhere to go to find it. I was never setting foot back where I grew up, so I had to find other ways.

What a mission! I have never walked so much in my life. I was sent from pillar to post. I went all over South Africa trying to prove that I am who I say I am.

We had no car; I used trains and taxis. I walked this journey by myself, armed only with ambition and an affidavit my mother had signed and her identity document. Everywhere I went, they asked me about my father. The answer was standard, but still, I was greeted by blank stares. After weeks and weeks of frustrations and no direction, I finally received my identity document, and for the first time I felt as though I truly belonged. This was 1995, a year after South Africa's first democratic elections. I did not vote as I was under-age at the time. I was however at the voting polls and the mood was indescribable. The very first time that Black people could vote in their own ancestral land! I was moved, we were moved.

Upon finishing my matric, I had not applied to any tertiary institution. I knew that my mother would not afford to take me to university or college. We never had those kinds of discussions, but it was very clear. I never had anyone guiding me about career choices and what to do to be able to go to university. So, I did not know what was next for me post-matric, but I never lost my ambition to succeed. I was determined to make something of my life and it started with was a good set of matric results.

It was in the middle of January in 1996, after receiving my matric results, that I woke to the reality of my circumstances. My mother could not afford to send me to university. By now, my brother and my sister had already dropped out of school, but were not contributing to the household. My brother was involved with the wrong crowds and causing significant trouble that landed him in jail a couple of times.

I woke up one day and decided to catch the two-hour train ride from Orange Farm to Johannesburg city and braved the walk from the Park Station to Braamfontein, where the University of Witwatersrand was situated. I remember feeling so small as I walked into Senate House and overwhelmed by sheer admiration for those magnificent buildings. I was nervous.

It smelled like education and freedom. The number of people and the movement all around the university frightened me. It was big; I did not know where to go or who to speak to. I was still really just that insignificant little girl from the Transkei, but I kept my composure.

I saw many prospective scholars being accompanied by their parents, families, and they were walking from one building to the next, from one office to the other.

They seemed to have things under control. There was excitement in the air and a sense of achievement that they seemed to be exuding. I was scared, but I once again tapped into that undying self-belief. I reminded myself that no one knew where I came from in that sea of people. Not a single person knew that the only money I had in my pocket that day, was five rands to catch the train back home, or that I did not even have money for lunch or a cold drink.

I shook off the fear and walked tall. I queued up like all of them and nervously awaited my turn.

Hours later, my turn finally arrived. I reached the window and I told the lady that I wanted to enroll for studies, but that I did not know what I wanted to study. She asked me for the registration fee. I told her I did not have it, but that if she gave me the forms, I would go home and ask my mother to help me with them and ask her for the money. She was not impressed, and told me I was wasting her time and that of the other people.

She told me to step out of the line. With tears in my eyes, I respectfully stepped out of the line, but sat back down on the same bench I was on all day. As the day came to an end, she realised I had not moved. I was so hungry that it felt as if I was on a hunger strike. She finally gave in and handed me the forms, but still I did not know what I was going to study or how I was going to pay for it.

After many days of catching the five am train in order to be amongst the first in the queue, the university accepted me. Part of the process included a consultation with a career counselor. I knew exactly the kind of person I was, and what I was passionate about, even at that tender age. I had great results and could have picked any course.

I told him how I loved working with people and that I really wanted to understand society and how it functions. I wanted to know what drives people. I was really telling him that I wanted to know why my mother made the decisions that she made and stuck by them, even when she knew we were hurting. I wanted to know why my father never came for me. I wanted to know why the people who could nurture me and give me a good upbringing chose not to and instead did everything they could to break me. I had so many questions, but I packaged my answer to him nicely. He helped me enroll for a Social Sciences degree. I chose Psychology and majored in Sociology and Social Anthropology.

I also decided to study English. It was a very bizarre choice at university, unless you planned on pursuing Linguistics or Literature. I did English to give myself the confidence to hold a conversation, comfortably.

English is an incredibly difficult language and I grew up in a world where no one spoke it every day. It was a medium of delivery at school, but it was not a language we spoke at all. Even our teachers would switch to IsiXhosa to explain an English lesson if we were not getting it.

You were also considered to be trying to be white if you spoke English. My dreams were larger, so I knew what I needed to do to be a versatile person. I equipped myself.

This was great, but there was the question of money to pay for all this. My mother did not have it. Lectures started, and everything started to come together.

I started to make a few friends. I was starting to feel as if I was a part of the community. I lived in one of the residences, too, albeit just outside the campus. This was one of the reasons I had to keep coming back to the university for eight weeks every morning to queue up for my spot in the sun. I had to stay at campus. There was no way I was going to stay with my mother. My dream was beckoning and I needed to set it up for success.

I could not take living with my mother, her new husband and my out of hand siblings. It was interfering with my state of mind. I often could not hear myself think from all the fights and screams. I still slept on the floor, and I would just bury myself on the other side of the bed on my grass mat and study until I fell asleep. I could not wait to get out of there.

Often, my teenage sister would cry out for her

father. One night, I decided to join in and ask for the whereabouts of my father. It was maybe the biggest mistake of my young life. My mother chased us out of the house in the night, but not before she beat the daylights out of us – she even slammed a bottle against my sister's head.

That drove me nuts! I thought she was going to kill her. She was frustrated and had no answers for us.

We were just frustrated and needed answers.

The missing middle

I loved Social Sciences; it gave me what I was looking for. Not in the obvious sense, but I learnt some key principles about life and society. I learnt about nature vs. nurture. I learnt about accountability and responsibility for our actions. I learnt about cause and effect. I learnt about ownership and decisions for our lives. I was so enthusiastic about the nuances of society and cultures. I felt as though I was growing.

I soon found Psychology boring because it did not tell me what I wanted to know. I dropped it after two years and carried on with my major, but I did find the nature vs. nurture debate to be an intriguing one, both in Psychology and Sociology. It was very relevant to me.

I will not in any way attempt to deal that subject here, but let me take a moment to explain, albeit briefly.

It is an ongoing debate about how humans develop physical, mental, and emotional traits unique to them. The nature side of this debate argues that people are products of a genetic timeline in which evolution and other characteristics have molded all of their ancestors and that you are the final product of that timeline.

According to nature, all of your characteristics such as the way you look, the way you feel, the emotions you experience, are already inside of you via genetic code and are turned on and off by your biological clock. Evidence that found this to be true is a study that found language is gained through the use of an inborn language acquisition device, Chomsky(1965).

On the other side of this argument, is the people who believe you are born with certain genetic characteristics, such as height, eye color, and so forth, but for the most part, you are born with a blank slate which is filled by your environment. This environment includes all the physical, mental, and emotional instances you are exposed to from the time you are born. The stimulation your brain receives from environmental interaction is what shapes you as you grow and learn. You are constantly learning, especially when you are an infant, and all this knowledge of your surroundings mould you.

Love and affection from other people are vital, too. In a 1977 study, Albert Bandura found that aggression is learned from the environment through imitation and observation.

The nature versus nurture debate raises philosophical questions about determinism and free will. This always captivated me. Free will to me, represented the power to choose, to decide, which I believe is innate in all of us.

Kendra Cherry recently wrote that nature refers to all of the genes and hereditary factors that influence who we are—from our physical appearance to our personality characteristics. Nurture, on the other hand, refers to all the environmental variables that impact who we are, including our early childhood experiences, how we were raised, our social relationships, and our surrounding culture.

Sarah Mae Sincero writes that each of these sides have good points and that it's really hard to decide whether a person's development is predisposed in their DNA, or a majority of it is influenced by their life experiences and the environment. As of now, we know that both nature and nurture play important roles in human development, but we have not known yet whether we are developed majorly because of nature or due to nurture.

In their Open Educational Resources, Lumen Learning say that today, developmental psychologists rarely take such polarized positions (either/or) with regard to most aspects of development; instead, they investigate the relationship between innate and environmental influences (both/and). They will often use the bio psychosocial model to frame their research: this model states that biological, psychological, and social (socio–economical, socio–environmental, and cultural) factors all play a significant role in human development. This resonates with me, but I also add spirituality to the debate, which for me, fuels your hope to make the right decisions.

We are all born with specific genetic traits inherited from our parents, such as eye color, height, and certain personality traits. Beyond our basic genotype, however, there is a deep interaction between our genes and our environment: our unique experiences in our environment influence whether and how particular traits are expressed, and at the same time, our genes influence how we interact with our environment (Diamond, 2009; Lobo, 2008). There is a reciprocal interaction between nature and nurture as they both shape who we become, but the debate continues as to the relative contributions of each.

One of the other queues I had to brave and embrace was the financial assistance queue. This was the place where children like me came to plead for assistance. I felt right at home. We became a small community of ambitious children, trying to chase their dreams.

After about six months of not paying fees, I was given the financial exclusion letter. I was told not to come back to the university the following semester and that I would also not receive my results. I was shattered. I tried everything I could and just never gave up.

I kept going to the financial aid office to check my

status and the situation was dire. One day, I decided to just go one last time before I left campus for good.

I broke down to my knees and howled when I was told I had been selected for financial assistance. It took that long, because I had to prove that I was the least fortunate compared to others in the same queue. My persistence and perseverance also stood me in good stead, as I seemed to have skin in the game.

I had a working parent, so it was that much harder to prove I was more needy than other children who did not. I was not needy enough, but not rich enough either. I was what is now coined the *missing middle.*

After numerous attempts, I was free. I felt overwhelmed with emotion. I went to my room and I cried uncontrollably. I finally had a shot at my dreams. I was determined to make a success of my life. I was going to grab this opportunity with both hands. I had so much to prove, especially to myself.

Well on my way: The vision

For the next couple of years, I worked very hard to excel at my studies. There were disruptions. Being at university was a whole new experience. Everything completely depended on me. I could do what I wanted with my time, but I had to be clear about my priorities.

I had always been a hard worker and a very diligent student. I developed a routine that would also allow me to have a little fun. We would hit the clubs on the nights I was not working, until wee hours of the morning. We just had enough time to go home to shower and go to lectures. Fun was clean then at least ours was. We did not always welcome advances.

No one from my family ever came to visit me. But I had a great bunch of friends who would come and drag me out of my room to take me to the nearest hang out spot. I started playing snooker. I was mean at it, and soon started playing tournaments. It was a very exciting time and I felt that I had grown to belong.

Other times, I would hide myself in the library just to push my studies. I knew what it took for me to be there and I could not jeopardise that opportunity.

A number of people where shocked that I graduated. I found that puzzling. They confessed that I partied so hard they never thought I would graduate. People never see the hard work you put in. Well, I did graduate even finishing my degree with six months to spare.

Some of the conditions of the loan were working back a portion during school holidays. I did. I did some of the most unglamorous work I had ever undertaken. I would file glass slides with blood at the Medical Research Council.

Every time I felt sorry for myself, I would gently remind myself to stay on course and keep focused on the goal. I also worked on weekends to earn some extra money. I belonged to an agency that found work for students like me.

For most of my time at university I distributed pamphlets at busy traffic intersections, promoted new products or new perfumes, and stock taking at supermarkets was a staple job for me.

I also found myself a job as a barista in one of the coffee shops in upmarket Killarney and Hyde Park. I would go to class in the morning, library at two in the afternoon, after my final tutorial for about three hours. Then, I would don my sneakers and went off to work where I would be on my feet and happily serving our faithful customers until wee hours of the morning.

I was chasing my dream. A friend of mine used to

tell me how much she admired my tenacity and ability to humble myself and do really unflattering jobs. She refused to stoop that low. What alternative did I have? I could not be more important than my dreams. Pride comes before a fall, and boy have I seen them fall by the wayside.

I also worked as a hand model for one of the premier modeling agencies. I just was not tall enough for the modeling contracts but the scout saw my hands and she was blown over. I had so many gigs but those were long term investments as we only got monies after three months. My hands made it onto the international brands stages but I only cared that they were helping me build a decent life.

The other condition of the financial aid was to pass all your subjects. If you failed a semester, the loan would be taken away – no negotiations would be entered into. There were other needy children who could benefit from the privilege. There was also a reward if you passed all your subjects; forty percent of the loan would be converted to a bursary, and you would not have to pay that back. The rest had to be paid back when you started working.

I proudly fulfilled all these requirements. I carried on and completed my degree. I earned myself a certificate of excellence as the best third-year student in my majors. I was automatically accepted to do my Honors.

I had a really tough decision to make: carry on, or start working and build some kind of life for myself and help my mother out?

I could not take up that opportunity, as I had to start working to support my family. I was overwhelmed when I finished paying my loan and still had a credit, because I over paid. I donated that back to the fund. It was not much, but it meant the world to me.

I was very grateful to TEFSA – now NSFAS – for the chance to fight for a dignified life. My life was only just beginning.

Cracked but not broken

As a young woman growing up, I refused to believe I would amount to nothing. If anything, I had a strong drive to prove to myself that was not my destiny. I had endless turmoil and internal conflict as a child because I knew I was destined for success but nothing in my environment encouraged that.

People who were supposed to care for me did all they could to break me. I did not break. It may have taken years of therapy to deal with the pain of not having my mother and father there to protect me, but I had to persevere in order to realise my personal goals. I had a lot of work to do.

Mandy Bibo in the article *Stages of Healing from Childhood Sexual Abuse*, writes about the stages that are necessary for healing. She says these may not be necessary for all survivors but are cornerstone of healing:

- The Decision to Heal

  Once one recognises the effects of sexual abuse in one's life, one needs to make an active commitment to heal. Deep healing happens only when one chooses it and is willing to change.

- The Emergency Stage

  Beginning to deal with memories and suppressed feelings can throw your life into utter turmoil. This is only a stage. It won't last forever.

- Remembering

  Many survivors suppress all memories of what happened to them as children. Those who do not forget the actual incidents often forget how it felt at the time. Remembering is the process of getting back both memory and feeling.

- Believing It Happened

  Most adult survivors often doubt their own perceptions. Coming to believe that the abuse really happened, and that it really hurt, is a vital part of the healing process.

- Breaking Silence

  Most adult survivors kept the abuse a secret in childhood. Telling another human being about what happened is a powerful healing force that can dispel the shame of being a victim.

- Understanding That It Wasn't the Victim's Fault

  Children usually believe the abuse is their fault.

Adult survivors must place the blame where it belongs – directly on the shoulders of the abusers.

- Contacting the Child Within

  Many survivors have lost touch with their own vulnerability. Getting in touch with the child within can help one feel compassion for self, more anger at the abuser, and greater intimacy with others.

- Trusting Oneself

  The best guide for healing is one's own inner voice. Learning to trust one's own perception, feelings, and intuition forms a new basis for action in the world. As children being abused, and later as adults struggling to survive, most survivors haven't felt their losses. Grieving is a way to acknowledge pain, let go, and move into the present.

- Anger

  Anger is a powerful and liberating force. Whether one needs to get in touch with it or has always had plenty to spare, directing rage squarely at the abuser, and at those who didn't protect the victim, is pivotal to healing.

- Disclosures and Confrontations

  Directly confronting the abuser and/or one's

family is not for every survivor, but it can be a dramatic, helpful tool.

- Resolution and Moving On

   As one moves through these stages again and again, one will reach a point of integration. Feelings and perspectives will stabilise. One will come to terms with the abuser and other family members. While one won't erase history, one will make deep and lasting changes in life. Having gained awareness, compassion, and power through healing, one will have the opportunity to work toward a better world.

It was not until I was almost forty, that I started telling my extended family what had happened to me. It took many years before I started talking about the abuse I suffered. I decided to share my story, because I knew there were many more people like me who have endured so much pain and suffering and who continue to struggle.

There are plenty children out there going through exactly what I went through, an even larger number perhaps of people who feel that they are gripped in the cycle of 'once abused, always an abuser'.

I am here to tell you it can be done. You can break free, but it is going to take everything you have.

I used to cry myself to sleep most of my young adult life. My daily prayer was for God to make me a better person. I prayed to God to grant me the ability to be at peace with my life. Above all, I prayed to God to help me deal with the contempt and severe disappointment I felt towards my mother.

She was actively trying to play a role in my life. She would help me financially whenever she could while I was at university. One day, she surprised me with a car, a Fiat Uno. Her colleague was emigrating so she got a good deal for four thousand rands. That was a pleasant surprise.

It was very strange to accept something from her. She was there, but all she represented to me was pain, rejection, and abandonment. I gracefully accepted it. It helped a lot with getting to work and also, it was good for my social life. It was really nice of my mother to do that for me.

I concluded through my journey that sometimes, there are no obvious answers. Instead of asking why, I started embracing *why not*. Who else would I have chosen this life for? Why not me? I had to find the reasons that I was chosen to walk this journey. I said to God, *surely you have a plan right!*

What were all these things for if not a grand plan? I stood firm and stayed focused, knowing that there was a purpose larger than just breathing. I knew I had to work hard to be something that others could look up to. I wanted to stand for hope.

I had a very clear vision of the fibre of my life. I

had to work hard to make that a reality. I was a big person now; I was responsible for my own life. The days of hanging on to what my mother did or did not do, were fast coming to expire.

Sadly, my mother was the only parent that even dared to show, but to me, she was the source of all my pain. At the time, I was just searching for something comforting from her; just a word that could make it all better, but that never came. I was hurting, but I was also busy building a life for myself. The pain had become such a big part of my life for so long, it was normal.

I remember when I was at university, I was sent to the now Archbishop Thabo Makgoba of the Anglican Church for counseling. He obtained his Masters in Educational Psychology at the university, but was also a part-time lecturer around the time I was there. He was also the chaplain of the university. They referred to him as the healer, and he really had a way of making you feel as if you were the chosen one. I had so many demons; they had to call in the big guns! I still laugh at myself when I think about this. You have to be able to laugh at yourself. This is how I get by, for real.

The archbishop really helped me with my spiritual outlook on life. I had started hating church, because my mother would force me to go. I hated that, but I never lost my spirituality. In fact, I felt that the church was hindering my progress.

I could not relate to the judgment that some Christians were so eager and quick to pass. I did not like the superiority that some churches displayed towards those who did not believe. I started questioning the interpretation of the bible by the church leaders.

He helped me embrace the purpose of my life. He helped me remember that I did not stumble upon this life, but that God chose me for it. Mine was to unlock that power within and let God lead me to my purpose. I walked away from our sessions encouraged and I hung onto those words and my spirituality until this day.

Tasting real life

The day I graduated from university was the happiest day of my life. It felt as though a huge rock had been lifted off my shoulders. I knew and believed that I was going to be all right. I had this great belief that my life was looking up. I did not go back home to my mother's house after university.

I stayed at a commune in Sandton, Johannesburg, with a bunch of crazy white people. That was the most fun I had ever had in my life. I learnt to let go and let my spirit free.

The best was when we all danced naked in the rain celebrating the start of a new year. The music was blasting and we were just so happy.

I love diversity. I thrive when I am experiencing different energies. My Social Sciences training was spot on in fueling my passion, and this was going to be even more apparent in the rest of my life and career.

I had started working in the call center of an employee benefits company. We were handling pension payout queries. I knew right from the start that this was not going to be for a long time, but I just needed corporate work experience.

I did not like my boss at all. She was very mean and only cared about the seconds someone took longer to pick up the next call. I found the job very draining, as I would have pensioners complaining and crying that they had not been paid their pension. Some walked for kilometers just to reach the pay point, only for them to not receive their benefit. I really did not like that, as most times, I felt helpless. I relied on people to help me solve the problem but often, the solution was not immediate.

It was not always the company's fault, but a family was negatively impacted either way. I learnt to work with people I did not like – especially my boss, but I respected her position.

I learnt to be empathetic; above all, I gained some much-needed work experience. I left three months later.

Prior to my departure, I was chatting to a family friend about my situation. I told him I was on the market looking for another job. He asked me to join his company that did project management. I thought *okay, sounds like a plan.*

I would start from the bottom as a junior, doing project administration. I loved it the moment I set foot into a training room. I attended what was the best project management academy at the time. I received training from basic all the way to advanced, long before

I even had the experience. I was always eager to shadow other facilitators and project managers. I always volunteered for extra work.

It was not long before I was placed at a client, doing project management office administration.

I watched seasoned project managers in action and I just knew that this was where I was meant to be. This was the career I was meant to follow. The ability and the opportunity to deliver through people was just so attractive to me.

I saw how much joy it brought to the team to deliver a tangible result, having started from nothing. I could identify with this. This was like a soundtrack to my life. I observed team dynamics and how the project leads or managers would handle them. I had strong opinions at times, and would forget I was still junior. I would advise the seniors on how I believed they should have handled a situation. Some took it well; others just saw me as an irritating bug that needed to be squashed.

It was not long before the clients I was placed at asked to take me on permanently, and also offered me a promotion. That was the beginning of my financial services career and the start of a magnificent career in project management.

On the personal front, I made a conscious decision to start living. I decided I was not my mother or my father's mistakes. I could not let that define me. Those were decisions that they made that led to unsavory outcomes, but I am not them.

From that day on, I decided that only I am responsible for my life. I wished they were there when I was younger and I needed them, but they were not. I could not change that.

I decided I could not let the shame of the abuse steal my joy. I decided I was going to talk about my hardship, I was going to share my story in order to give others hope. I wanted them to know where I had come from and that I was still standing. I felt free – liberated! – but first, I had to consolidate this newly found state of being through working with counselors, psychologists, and coaches. I went to work.

Love deeply longed for, never came

When I was twenty-three years old, my mother insisted on talking to me about my childhood. I really could not, because I was just so afraid of what she would say. I could not trust her with my heart. I did not want her to see me crying and I could not let her see my weakness.

I did not want her to see that out of all of them, she is the one that really broke my heart. To me, all the pain I suffered was because of her absence. It is intriguing how, as a child, your world is modeled on your mother being a saint, your savior.

Other people may have done what may be deemed the worst things to be done to a child, but somehow, I believed that they had that chance because she was not there. I was convinced then, even as a young adult, that she could have made it all stop; that she could have prevented it. At the most, she could have come for me when she became aware of the abuse.

Growing older, I learnt that life is not that basic. Having a mother and father does not guarantee you safety, protection, and love. They could be the ones inflicting all the pain. I also learnt that some people have had wonderful extended families who cared for and nurtured them even better than their own parents could have. So, which is better, really?

I started having many conversations with myself about the relationship between a child and a parent. I had even more questions and deep thoughts about the relationship between a mother and a child; even deeper thoughts about the role destiny plays in that equation.

I once said in one of my talks that because your mother gave birth to you, does not guarantee that they will love you; it does not guarantee that they will protect you or even want anything to do with you.

A lady came up to me afterwards in tears, and she said to me that had to be the most heart-breaking thing she had ever heard. We talked about it. I said, *"Is it possible that my mother's role in my life was to just deliver me safely into this earth so that God could put me to work?"*

This line of thinking just dragged me to another place, my life was unraveling. Perhaps this was just the way it had to be. I had more questions than answers again, but I felt as if I was making a breakthrough, in my own way.

My mother persisted. I eventually gave in and decided to go and hear what she had to say. It was a very painful process. It was worse than I had feared.

Perhaps this is the one and only time in my life so far that the one thing I feared the most, did in fact happen. I got to find out on that day that same things that happened to me, also happened to my sister, and we both never knew. My mother also admitted to knowing what used to happen to us.

That took me aback. I cried, a lot, painfully so. She said she could not come for us, because she had no means to look after us. What do you say to that?

That was a very bad day for me. I told her the price of that plate of food and roof over our head was too high. I told her I would have slept under the bridge if it meant I could be with her and be protected from all that abuse. This meeting did not really make things better, but it brought me closer to a significant reality about decisions and consequences.

I started thinking that my mother took the easy way out, like my father did. She was just twenty-six years old when she had me; three children seemed like a heavy burden for her, so she took the easy way out. What kind of woman gives birth to three children and then feeds them to the wolves?

I was hurt, disappointed, and I felt let down by an excuse I could not fight back. I had so much internal turmoil, but my life had to carry on.

Another thought I wrestled with was, *what if my mother really never knew how to be a mother?* She herself never had a mother.

What if she really believed she was making the right decision? What if it was the right decision? After all, many other children were being raised by extended families. What was the worst that could have happened to us?

I contemplated the idea of ever having children and right then I decided that I would opt out of motherhood because "I did not want to screw my children up". I felt that it was a generational curse. Still, at no point did I ever feel sorry for myself. I had a clear grip on my reality and I was working on getting out of this state.

Anyway, at some point I bought the story about the lack of means to look after us. I worked out when she had started working. My mother did not struggle much for work – at least it was not for very long. She found work, but never came back. That is the point at which I always became stuck, and the answers never came.

There was the matter of my brother. My mother always had a soft spot for him. To her, he was perfection personified. He let her down on so many occasions. I guess as any mother would have it, she never gave up on him. Unfortunately, she was also enabling his ways. We would quarrel a lot over this.

I would support my family financially as much as I could. The demands kept coming and it is not as though I was earning much. As the years went on, I just felt that I was being taken advantage of. The only time any of my family members spoke to me, was when they wanted money. It caused a huge rift between my brother and I.

It took a very long time but I just could not keep feeding his needs anymore. Sadly, he was not only using the money for food.

Can I really take another stabbing?

I remember one day I was at my mother's house for the 2004 April holidays. My brother came around and I could see he was off, but paid no attention. He left and came back later that day in a drunken state. He pulled a knife on me. I was shocked!

He was mumbling something about how I told his wife that he was useless and I wondered why she married him. Lies, lies, and more lies. I kept explaining to him that I never even spoke to his wife. It mattered not what I said; he was on a mission to hurt me.

He chased me around the house for hours, trying to stab me. My mother and her husband protected me. He would not let up.

There was way more to it than he was letting on. He was pissed off that I refused to give him money. He was angry that I gave my mother a car and not him. He was mad at the success I was able to achieve. He seemed to have forgotten that he made the decision to drop out of school and become involved with the wrong crowd.

He was my brother, I would have always ensured

that he had food in his mouth, but even I had a line; especially as it started being detrimental to my own financial health.

It took four hours for the police to come. This was just the township and priorities were not given to those communities. They escorted me out of my mother's house, but not before my brother had stabbed my stepdad on his arm.

I was so heartbroken. I sunk into a dark place for a while. I just felt so alone, all over again. He was the closest I ever got to having a father, he was my big brother. I feared him from there on. That was essentially the end of my relationship with him. Things were never going to be the same. I also wondered if I actually ever had a relationship with him, if so, how was it ever benefitting me?

A week earlier, a very close family friend had the same experience. Her younger brother attacked her older brother at her mother's house. Sadly, he stabbed him to death right there on his mother's floor. It was the hardest thing to take. So, I had every right to be worried and concerned for my life. Seems knives were chasing me everywhere I went, but I was still standing and I was grateful to have walked away with my life still intact.

This fight with my brother unfortunately also unleashed a flurry of emotions that I had towards my mother and how she had raised my brother. I felt she had enabled this. He never apologised for what he did. Yes, I know all about forgiving people even when they do not ask for forgiveness, because it is good for you and your own peace of mind. It is also great for people to just apologise.

For years after that, my mother would force him down my throat. To be fair, she was trying to encourage us to reconcile. Unfortunately, she was never going to win. She always took his side and even with this, she did.

She made me out – once again – to be the monster that does not forgive.

Everyone must own their actions and live with the consequences. I moved on from the incident, but I was never going to trust him again. I was terrified of him, knowing things he had done to others and how he was living his life.

My relationship with my mother grew more strained over time. I shut out the noise and focused on myself. I worked on my own healing process. I wanted to be left alone, but that was wishful thinking. I had built up so many walls around me, especially when it came to my mother. I needed the walls because I was still under attack.

I was still just that little girl who needed her mother, who longed for her love and protection. She was forcing a relationship that was not there. I also felt that my mother had ignored me all those years and used up all her energy on the two children who turned out to be more of a burden than she had anticipated. I would become so furious when she would tell me how she raised me and sent me to school.

I felt she was claiming glory she did not deserve. She was laying a claim to something she had no right claiming. All I ever wanted from her was love and protection. I never received that in my formative years and in the years after, but I believed that I was worthy of it all. The fact that I did not receive it, did not cast a spell on me. I was worthy of it. So, I decided to give it to myself.

That lack of a strong sense of belonging was still a lingering deficiency. This is one of the things I had to work on. I had to be okay with the fact that I really had no strong family roots.

My father and his whole family never existed to me. For many years, I thought about looking for him, but I was much older and really thought that if he wanted to be my father he would have found me. His family could have found us, but they did not. I had no information to go with; my mother said he never knew where he was. I have never known what it is like to have a father, but that was not going to define me.

I decided to define my own sense of belonging. I made the decision that I was enough and that I was happy to rather charter the path on my own than be with people that did not have my best interests at heart.

I became okay with being alone. I no longer feared the silence in my life. I embraced the emptiness and the spaces.

It took a lot of work and sheer bravery to just sit in my pain and become acquainted with it. Deep in that pain, I found the little girl, and I embraced her. I told her it was okay to cry, and I promised to always look after her. I filled the dark and empty spaces with wholesome things in my life.

I grew a nice set of wonderful friends who inspired me to better. I became involved with charity work so that I could forget about my own pain and focus on making other people's lives better. I felt the growth. I was still standing in spite of it all.

At no point in my life have I ever questioned the reason I was born. I grew to also accept that God chose me for this journey. My path to the life I now live had to be exactly as it was supposed to be for impact.

I can now speak with authority on fighting against all odds and jumping every hurdle in life to prosper. I never even for one second believed that I would amount to nothing. I did not doubt my God–given abilities. I grew into my purpose.

The more I talk to people, the more they find healing, courage, and comfort. They look at me and believe, without a doubt, that if I could come out on the other side, so can they. I represent hope. This is the life I was meant to live.

I developed a great sense of self with a very strong internal compass. Even today, I continue to pray for God's wisdom, for direction, and for him to help me become a better person each day because it is very easy to revert back to anger and develop hatred. I am not about that life.

I also put into action my plan and love for travel. I realised I was meant to travel when I was at university.

Margaret Mead intrigued me when I studied Social Anthropology. As an anthropologist, Mead was best known for her studies of the non-literate people of Oceania, especially with regard to various aspects of psychology and culture. As a celebrity, she was most notable for her forays into such far-ranging topics as women's rights, child rearing, sexual morality, nuclear proliferation, race relations, drug abuse, population control, environmental pollution, and world hunger. She travelled to some of the most remote places in the world to study societies; cultures, and the introduction to her tickled my curiosity.

I decided then that this would be a big part of my life. I must say that my Anthropology professor did certainly not ignite my intrigue with her.

I remember the first time I stepped onto an airplane. I was twenty-three years old. I worked for a bank and I was in charge of a conference in Durban and Cape Town. I had to travel to those locations, and I was clueless. I did not know how to put on a seatbelt.

I actually knew absolutely nothing about flying. I had a really considerate colleague who took me under her wing. She was really nice to me. Often labelled a racist and intolerant, I wondered why she took such a keen interest in me.

Our seats were in business class, so this made it even more daunting. She sat next to me and showed me how to put on my seat belt and taught me all the important things about safety. I heard none of it, because I was so terrified. She held my hand as we took off and I took it from there on. Like a pro, I kept praying for safe landing.

I started travelling outside South Africa, but within the Southern African region. I loved Mozambique the most. It is still a top favorite.

My big trip came in 2004. I had just sold my first property at a good profit. I used the money for a deposit of my second property, new furniture, and appliances.

The biggest spend was my first trip to Europe. I was twenty-six years old and booked a tour of twelve countries with other young adults under thirty-five. I thought there would be more over twenty-fives than I encountered but I was the oldest.

Most group members came from Australia, New Zealand, Canada and China. Twenty-year olds from Australia bullied me. They knew how to do a number on you when they were drunk. It was not worth my effort, but it was a rude awakening. I was the oldest and the only black person in a bus of about thirty people living together and travelling together over a couple of weeks.

I seem to always go about life the hard way. I always waited until the next day to confront them and they would run for the woods.

It was a fantastic adventure. I had the time of my life. Outside of the rude little creeps from Australia, I connected with amazing young people. The Chinese group always kept to themselves. There was a group of three Capetonians who also kept to themselves. I really enjoyed the Canadians; very chilled people who kept apologising for the Aussies' rudeness. Through that experience, I decide that my children – if I ever had any – would be well-travelled at a very young age. This is the way of life I wanted for them, but first I had to grasp it at a not-so young age according to world script.

Most of the people on the tour were on a gap year. This was and still is a tradition in most countries where once you finish high school you go travelling for a year. I always think about the practicalities of this kind of life in a country like ours, where the majority of the people live below the poverty line. Whilst they would find odd jobs, their parents financed their trips. There were a very few who really had to find work in order to cover the rest of their costs during their gap year.

I have been travelling ever since. It may have taken a while, but I had to work very hard for it. It did not matter how long it took me but I had a clear goal. I have been to many more countries since; some multiple times. I've enjoyed many more adventures, but above everything, I have recently been able to do so with my young children.

I have always wanted them to experience diversity, which South Africa has in abundance. Unfortunately, very few people appreciate the value of this in our country. Our differences have been and continue to be used against us. I take my children to foreign worlds where they can learn to be comfortable with different people and ways of life unlike theirs. I want them to seek diversity. I want them to find the thrill in befriending people from all walks of life.

I am also very fortunate to have them attend the school that they do, because there are many children who come from outside the country and they make friends across the spectrum with absolutely no hang-ups. The ability to help them have a life with multiple perspectives has been one of my greatest achievements.

My recent adventures took us to the Scandinavian countries. There were so many highlights, including cruising from Stockholm to Helsinki on a majestic cruise liner, the Silja Symphony. As we arrived in Helsinki we sampled some moose meatballs and reindeer sausages at the market square.

What an experience! We also went to Prague, Vienna and ended off with an incredible stop-over in Dubai at The Atlantis.

I feel most blessed when my children are having new experiences and I am right by their side with my husband in tow. The growth we experience as a family on these trips is second to none.

One of our previous trips included Geneva, Chamonix, Santa Margherita Ligure, Porto Fino, Milan, Rome, and a final stop in Paris, starting in Disneyland. This was an incredible trip. We watched snow start to come down the mountains into the gorgeous skiing town of Chamonix in France – such a magical experience!

I ticked an all-time bucket list item with Porto Fino and San Fruttuoso in Italy. I became a child at Disneyland, something that took me by surprise. Tears rolling down my face, I went on every ride. For the first time in my life, I was a child. I gave myself permission to go full throttle on the experience.

I shared with my family how I was feeling. That was a very emotional time for me, in a very good way. We continue to look for more adventures as a family.

I do also enjoy the occasional solo-travel. Whether it is for business or leisure, I take full advantage of exploring the world and just having some time to myself.

I went off to Florence, Italy to gain some inspiration to complete this book. There was no better place to go for some solitude time. You are never short of inspiration in Florence.

The purpose driven life

I worked very hard and with dedication and commitment to grow my career. I moved up the ladder rather swiftly in my corporate career. I was presented with many opportunities to work with diverse people from all walks of life. I have always been thrusted into situations where I was in the minority and I had to find a way to be successful regardless. I remember the time a white girl at work asked me, "jokingly" if I had slept with someone important to be gaining so much success. It was not a joke of course but those were common utterances in my years in corporate. I just always felt sorry for them. You must be feeling so small to believe that another woman's success is a result of sexual favours. What does that say about you?

I have a simple philosophy in life. We all have the same dreams, we share the same fears, and we want to be happy, healthy, and have happy children.

We want to do meaningful work, we all want to feel valued and relish the opportunity to contribute to society.

I always treat people with dignity and respect. I

give them a chance to prove themselves as I would have them do unto me. I cannot work within settings where everything is vanilla. I feel stifled when independent thinking and initiative is not allowed. I am also really resolute and highly opinionated.

Throughout my career I have viewed people through this lens. This has equipped me with great human interaction skills. I value relationships above everything else. I am in awe of what the human spirit can achieve.

I decided I was going to dedicate the years into honing my skills and becoming the best project manager I could be. I was nominated for multiple project managers awards much earlier in my career; these accolades were bestowed upon me by industry colleagues. It gave me validation that I was on the right track.

It was not easy. Your ability to influence people to see the big picture is tested and makes all the difference. You have to know when to be hard and when to nurture. I could not have been more grateful for my Social Sciences training.

There was a time when doing a Masters in Business Administration (MBA) was fashionable. Companies were sponsoring big monies for the qualification. Many times, I was approved for funding, but I decided not to pursue it. I was so focused on becoming the best in my career that I felt that the qualification would distract me from my goals. So, I instead studied within my profession and became certified as a professional project manager. I can assure you, it was the best decision I could have ever made.

As I grew in my career and in stature, I found myself with an unexpected internal conflict.

I was very successful. I was getting opportunities even though I did not have a post-graduate degree. Remember, I sacrificed my Honors to start working and support my family. I had also foregone the MBA in order to focus on honing my skills and being there for my children.

The higher I went up the ladder, the more insecure I felt about my education credentials. It bothered me for a while. In fact, I was bothered by the fact that it bothered me. I knew what it took to earn my undergraduate degree.

I was successful without that post graduate qualification. In fact, I was more successful than my peers. I was a specialist and a leader. I had domain experience and knowledge. Companies were falling over themselves to hire me, but I felt as though I would be exposed as inadequately educated.

I did however realise that, perhaps the insecurities came because I was gaining incredible success and the negative scripts in my childhood had started to creep up again. I felt I may not have been good enough and that I needed more credentials to cushion me.

I had to deal with my mental muscle again. I worked with a coach who helped me gain clarity of mind. The end result was the same: I had no interest in an MBA. I was one of the most qualified people in my field. I had enjoyed career and financial success without it. I was putting myself under unnecessary pressure. I did, however, end up doing a corporate education qualification that was a mini-version of the MBA. I gained the principles I perhaps needed to support my business acumen, however there was no significant uptick in my life as a result.

I snapped out of it. I stopped comparing myself to others. I acknowledged the many hurdles and decisions I had made that got me where I was. I appreciated the effort it took to grow myself.

Honestly it has become even more irrelevant for me. Once you have made a decision, embrace it and own it. There will always be someone more educated than you, someone who earns more money than you. You must be content with the direction you have chosen to take and the outcomes of your efforts. If not, change it, but never compare yourself to others. The lane you are on is the best lane for you.

The love bite; written in the stars

My social life was fabulous. I felt as if had really found my groove. I had always had family issues, so those never ceased, but I was busy building my life. Success was not going to find me crying in a corner. On the love front, I was very picky and very particular. I had no interest in settling for less than what I believed I deserved.

I had gained success and I was independent, living my life and travelling. I was enjoying my friendships and meeting new people. I always liked spending time with people who were completely different to me. I enjoyed exchanging ideas and getting philosophical about life, as you can imagine. I told myself early on that I would not stick around people that did not add value in my life. I still live by that, and I assume and hope they do, too. If you do not stimulate me intellectually or spiritually, then there is very little between us.

I also adore people who have a great sense of humor. I can laugh for days!

Naturally, I am drawn to people who have risen above all odds to reach their dreams. I cannot stomach people who play victim. I have never had that, in spite of my upbringing.

After many failed relationships, I was really in no mood for more. I was open to meeting people, but I was not looking for anything serious – just now they want to have children! I kept things casual for a while.

One sunny Sunday afternoon at the beginning of 2006, I had pulled into a carwash to have my car conditioned. It was a beautiful little BMW Z4, and I felt like a goddess in it. I would drop the top and enjoy beautiful summer days in my city; crisp air against my shaven head. I was living the life.

Whilst waiting in the queue to pay, I saw a gentleman coming up to me. The first thought that went through my mind was how brave he was. I was renowned for a very unfriendly demeanor. Apparently, I used to threaten a lot of suitors, so they would confess to me upon realising that I was a sweetie pie.

This man told me that he knew me from university, but I could tell he was nervous. I admired his courage to come up to me and ask for my number in the middle of a long queue. That is brave! I was polite, but not very eager. Still, he seemed okay, so I gave him my number.

Turns out he had already driven out of the garage when he saw me pulling in, and drove back to talk to me. Story goes that he had been trying to catch my attention over the years, but I was just too busy to notice.

One thing I had started to enjoy immensely, was travelling. I would go on solo trips around Southern Africa and I had started going to Mozambique with my friends. Life was peachy.

When I met him, I was planning a trip to Cape Town for my twenty-eighth birthday – a solo trip. He called me around then, and I just could not talk, so I promised to call him when I was free, but I forgot.

Months went on, and he would call. Eventually, I wanted to talk to him. He was so persistent and not pushy at all – very patient, so I started thinking about him, a lot.

I invited him on my next trip to Mozambique. It was great; we had a wonderful time and talked about everything. I felt comfortable. He was smart, cute, and had a great sense of humor. We shared a love for travel and talked about our next trip together. That was the beginning of a very special union.

I was interested. He had all the qualities I had wanted in a man. He came from a strong family background with lots of siblings, but they somehow remained close and their parents had done an amazing job raising them.

I still remained tentative, but very keen. The interest grew each day. I started realising that he was exactly what I had been holding out for, but I was still a bit skeptical about my ability to hold a proper relationship.

I was still a work in progress. I had just started on my journey to healing and I was concerned but I told myself that there are truly good people out there, and that I had grown to be able to differentiate them. I had to trust my instincts and give into this force that was starting to come over me. I told myself I deserve to be loved in spite of all that I had grown up with.

Some of the work I had started to put in was really about loving myself. Before you can truly love someone else, you have to actively learn how to love yourself. This is not just about caring for yourself; it also means showing yourself love each and every day. This is very difficult to master when you are still battling self-esteem issues.

I really like what Pamela Jacobs says in *5 Steps to Finding Love After Abuse*. She recommends that you think about all the ways you would show a new partner how you love him or her. You might buy them gifts, compliment them, spend time with them, or do nice things to show them you care. To love yourself, means to do all of those things – for you. Every day, practice treating yourself as if you are your newest, hottest love interest.

Treat yourself to things you love. Cook yourself nice meals. Go on dates with yourself.

She goes on to say that if you want someone to love you for who you are, you first have to do so yourself. And remember, you set the standard for how a future love interest will treat you. I have been very clear on this. Loving yourself is a necessity not a selfish act, as some would have you believe. You cannot give what you do not have.

I was also very clear about the partner I wanted to share my life with. Some of my friends used to tell me that my standards were too high and that I would never meet someone like that. I was happy to never than settle for less than what I believed I deserved.

You must decide what you want. So often, we accept whatever a partner has to offer us. Because of the messages we received that taught us we are only worthy if someone loves us, we have learned to lower our standards. But, as long as you don't know what you want, you will continue to meet and fall into relationships with people who do not fit in your life. It's critical that you become clear on what you want your life to look like, and how a potential partner would fit into that.

I knew my worth, even as I was transforming. I have always known that I deserved better. I knew I would find happiness someday, but I had to be able to realise that it was authentic and it had to have a strong foundation to land on. I deserved to be happy in spite of what I learnt from my abusive and neglected upbringing.

Six months later, we went on another trip together – this time tackling Asia. We went to Thailand,

Malaysia, Singapore, and stopover in the United Arab Emirates. This was the first time we were going to be away and staying together for such a long time. It was two-and-a-half weeks. I was anxious and very excited at the same time. He had to tell his family about this friend he is going overseas with, just in case I was a serial killer.

We had such an amazing time walking endlessly and exploring new worlds, talking away, and just getting to know one another. We were laying on the beach in Sentosa, an island off the coast of Singapore, when we started talking about our next trip. This is always a very exciting conversation; I live for the next vacation. Nothing much has changed.

Just as we were carrying on, he turned to me and said we can go on another trip or we could use the money to pay for a wedding. I sat calmly frozen for a while, and thought it was the daiquiris that got him talking funny.

We had only been dating a mere seven months.

I cannot think of a more romantic proposal for me. I suck at romance; I tend to be very practical.

The sunset in Sentosa seemed to be even more special. I was a bit confused, because I never wanted to get married. *So, why was I feeling a little tingly all over my body*? Why did this sound like the greatest idea I have ever heard? I said yes, without hesitation. I said yes!

We caught a flight out of Singapore to Bangkok

and I just kept starring at him. He must have thought, *what a weirdo!*

Upon our arrival, I held both his arms and I asked him to just stop. I looked him in the eyes and said "So, about yesterday?"

He smiled, looked at me, and said, "Yes?"

I asked if he meant it, and he said, "Of course!"

Right then, we started planning our wedding. We agreed on a date exactly twelve months from that day. We obviously still had to go home and meet the families and inform them.

I felt that was the happiest day of my life. It felt that I could finally start something of my own. Surprisingly, I had no fear in my bones, no doubt whatsoever. He was the one!

We returned home around the beginning of October and we just had so much to do. What seemed to be top of mind for him, was family planning. He wanted to start a family right after we were married. He spent his time doing research on it, and the time it could or may take for us to fall pregnant. Right there, instead of me running away for my life, I said "Absolutely!"

It was like an out-of-body experience. I was surprising myself everyday. I was in for the ride!

My future husband was busy bringing me all kinds of research about the impact of contraceptives if you had been on them for a very long time. I was twenty-eight and he was thirty-two. He told me he was ready to be a father the moment we were married.

I sweetly told him that the research might not apply to us. It could take longer, or not. Wait for it; I agreed to come off the pill to allow my body to return back to natural state in order for us to start a family the moment we were married.

We carried on planning the wedding. It was a very exciting time. We were making big decisions.

One day I caught myself in the mirror and I said "You are going to be a great mother, because you know what it is like to not have one."

It was the fourteenth of December of that very same year that I found out I was pregnant.

I kept telling my friend that I was not feeling great. I thought maybe I had too much champagne and needed to detox. I did, but nothing had helped. I would take cold showers because I felt so hot.

She suggested that I should stop by the pharmacy and buy a pregnancy test. I rubbished her claims and said I just needed to maybe detox again. But I gave in and took the tests – four of them and they all gave the same result.

We were going to be parents. I was going to be a mother.

He was ecstatic – over the moon! I was terrified!

I just had this major outburst. I panicked. We were not yet married; this is not how it was supposed to happen. The reality of the moment was overwhelming.

He tried to calm me down and re-assure me, but it did not help, because it was not about him. I now had to face up to my demons for real. He left me alone to go rejoice with his friends, which gave me time to take it all in.

I worked through my feelings. I felt more and more excited each day. I called a lunch with my friends and I broke the news to them before that year ended. Not even one of them got up to congratulate me, because they thought I was joking. Not a single one of the eight women took me seriously.

They only believed me weeks later when I sent them a note confirming we are expecting twins. Only then did they believe me. Who could blame them?

So, there I was, eight weeks pregnant when we found out – meaning I fell pregnant immediately. So, I was right; research did not apply to us. It was to remain the joke of our lives until this day.

I carried on planning the wedding, doing – you know – life.

There was family pressure on us to move up our wedding date so that our babies would be born within wedlock. We looked at one another and flat-out refused. We had nothing to be ashamed of. We were going to stick to our plans as they were.

The elders asked what we would tell the children when they are older and asking. We responded that we would not tell them anything but the truth. It is such a beautiful truth.

Let us just say the elders did not see our point, but it did not matter; it was between the two of us.

I told my mother who once said I hated her so much that I would never allow her near my children. This was not true. I have never hated my mother. I just did not have a relationship with her. I did not know her. I was angry at her at some point in my life, and rightfully so.

Our timing was out of sync. She wanted a relationship with me when I believed it was too late. We were always in conflict, but I never hated her. I wanted her to take full accountability for her actions and decisions. I wanted her to own what was hers. I wanted her to stop blaming others and playing the victim blaming people she trusted.

I needed her to tell me she was sorry. That never came, but she was still entitled to her grandchildren. It was their right to have a relationship with her, no matter our vibe. She was very happy.

The birth of my twin girls was as special as they are. It was at twenty-six weeks and five days that these little creatures decided they wanted to meet their mom and dad. It was way too early for them to come, but we were prepared.

We had an amazing gynecologist. Weighing a mere nine hundred and fifty and one thousand and eighty grams respectively, they had no business coming out that early. My little angels, my miracle babies, were born on the 11ᵗʰ of May, around Mother's Day!

I spent some quiet moments smiling, laughing, and talking to God. I told him he was so full of surprises, and frankly, that he pulled a fast one on me on Mother's Day. He was really going to force this healing process down my throat. All kinds of emotions came flooding back.

There was no medical reason for my babies to be born when they were born. They had no complications and they needed very little whilst in hospital. They just needed blood and to grow. Fortunately, their aunt was a match, and everything else was just about patience, care, nurturing, and growth.

I was soon discharged and had to make the daily drive to the clinic to look after my little ones. I was there every day when the morning shift changed, and when the evening shift started. I stayed there all day.

I completely forgot about my own healing process, and just focused on what I needed to do – nurturing my babies.

For two months and a week, they stayed in hospital, mostly in Intensive Care Unit (ICU) and High care due to their size. They had to be monitored closely.

I was there. I would change their miracle nappies and pour the breast milk into the tubes. I was the primary care giver; the nurses were supplementing and doing their jobs, but I was their mother.

Their father was also there, we were a family. I finally had my own – my very own – family. Something shifted in me.

It was a month into this new journey when I started feeling as if the walls were closing in on me. I did not feel great. I phoned my then husband to be and I told him how I was feeling. He immediately told me to fly out and join him in Cape Town, at our new home.

I told the sisters at the clinic. They all came and hugged me and told me I was the subject of their meetings. They were worried about me and were keeping a close eye on me. They were worried I had been pushing myself so hard since the day the babies were born and that I took no time to rest and look after myself, and heal.

I wept uncontrollably because I felt so guilty to be leaving them behind, but I needed to rest and recharge. I slept for three days, only waking up to eat and use the bathroom. I came back fully refreshed to look after my babies.

Blessed was the day they left the hospital and came home to us.

Three years later, we were blessed with a little boy who just stole all our hearts. I was not so lucky this time; he baked in that oven for a full term. I really got to experience pregnancy in all its grandeur.

My family was complete. My heart was full, but there were many scares with him.

I suffered multiple false alarms towards the end of the pregnancy. The nurses at the clinic always had me on regular walk-ins to monitor the contractions.

The days before he was born, I told my gynecologist that I was not feeling great. I felt overly heavy and extremely uncomfortable. I felt as if I was tearing early on the day he was born. Mine was a scheduled caesarian, so I was not waiting for labour.

I eventually went into theatre to give birth after nine months. All things looked familiar, except the hounding headache I suffered just after the anesthesiologist had administered the spine block. I told my gynecologist that I was not feeling good. She immediately told me to tell him exactly what was happening.

Firstly, I could not breathe. Then came an excruciating headache that got me so hysterical they had to drag my husband out of the changing room. I kept asking why they were drilling into my head. They all had their hands up and showed me they were nowhere near my head.

Something was obviously horribly wrong. I had always had a fear of dying on the operating table; only this time, I was being tortured before death.

I cannot think of anything worse than having seasoned and trusted specialist doctors doing their best to hide their fear whilst you are lying on an operating table. They had to quickly come up with another plan. I heard them discuss general anesthetic and discussing all sorts of pros and cons with that. It was like a movie or one of those medical series.

My husband just kept holding my hand and re-assuring me that no one was touching me, but my head still felt as if it was being drilled into. The planning took minutes, but it felt like hours to me.

My team of doctors was really incredible and they have looked after me from my very first children. So, I trusted them. I trusted my gynecologist to make the right call and the pediatrician to be ready for any eventuality. I really just trusted God to bring my husband and I through this ordeal. I just wanted my little boy to be healthy, no matter the price.

It typically takes fifteen to twenty minutes to close a caesarian wound. My very trusted, capable, highly competent, and smart gynecologist was now on about forty minutes. I could see the other doctors looking rather nervous.

My baby was out, healthy, and bouncy, so I had little to worry about, but still, I needed my gynecol-ogist's head to come up and tell me all was good.

I asked her what was going on. She told me I was right when I said I was tearing. My uterus had a sizeable tear and she had to repair that first before she could close the womb.

At recovery, she explained the whole thing to us again and finally said that, unfortunately, this means it would be too risky to try and have another baby. I thought this woman is mad!

I had just had the most traumatic experience, and she is talking about more children. I immediately said "It is well with my soul". My husband and I had already decided, prior to this ordeal, that this would be our last child.

I suffered severe migraines after the birth of my son, never having had a single migraine in my life prior. It took more than a year for them to subside.

My little guy was healthy, beautiful, and loved. The doctors, all, collectively, could not explain why I had such a reaction to the spine block. They had never seen that before. Well, I was still standing, barely but standing nonetheless.

Tragic losses, deep mourning

Speaking of births, my best friend, whom I had known for over twenty years, sadly, recently did not survive the birth of her twins.

She was in hospital on bed rest for a month. When I went to see her, she was in great spirits, and had a nail technician come to her ward and do her nails. She said, "I may be on bed rest, but my nails still have to look proper."

She was calm and at ease for a person that was cooped up in a tiny ward for a month. She told me she was not bothered, as she really wanted to deliver healthy babies. She was adamant.

My friend was a smart, driven, and very focused woman. She had run two Comrades marathons back-to-back. Her career was blossoming. She inspired me when she cashed out her pension and went to France to do her MBA. She had such clarity of mind and a big family soul. I always found inspiration in her.

She was a very small-built human being – dynamite in a small package. She had decided very early in her life that she would adopt a child. She fulfilled that goal when she received a gorgeous little man at birth. This time around, she was in a loving relationship that had all the signs of a great love. She was very happy, and they decided that giving birth to their very own child together would be a beautiful thing. They wanted a little sister or brother for their adopted little boy.

The last time I had visited her, I picked up flowers from the hospital shop and I really did not like them.

I was planning my day and working out which florist I would go to for fresh flowers one morning, when I received a call telling me there was sad news.

I immediately thought that the twins did not make it. I had not finished that thought when the caller told me "We lost her". I firstly did not understand who, and what she was talking about. I finally told her she was not making sense.

She repeated, "I am sorry Amanda but we have lost her". I had to stop on the side of the road, because I just could not carry on driving. I had never factored that into any possible or remote equation.

Just like that, my best friend had given birth to beautiful twin boys, bled out, and died a mere couple of hours later. It was a palpable sense of loss.

She was gone at thirty-eight years old. If I had secrets in my life, this was the girl to carry them. Whenever something great happened to me, she was the first call and I was hers.

The heavens opened, it was pouring the day we buried her, at the precise moment that her coffin was being lowered into the ground. I looked up and I said "only you could exit like that, my queen bee".

This was very difficult for me, because I had tragically lost a great friend, a brother to me, my business mentor, and my husband's best friend of thirty years a mere two months earlier. I started having to face my own mortality. The reasons for living and the suddenness of death consumed me. Two very young and significant people in my life, who had young families, had just vanished – just like that.

I have always lived by the philosophy of "You have one life. Live it as though tomorrow may never come", but I never thought that would be tested so brutally.

I had never experienced that much devastation in my life. Watching their young families, continues to be a great source of heartbreak for me but even then, we all have to keep living.

Life has just not been the same without them. I have not been the same without them, but I have found a way of rejoicing in the time and the memories we shared. It was also a stark reminder of how precious life is and how sudden death can be.

As you grow older, there are people in your life that you think and assume will always be there. These two were that for me. At no point did I ever think I would go through life without them, because of the significant roles they played. They were wonderful human beings, a big part of my pack. I miss them every day, and I was blessed to have them in my life.

You are the mother now

Mother's Day became a symbol of hope for me. I am reminded every year when all mothers are being celebrated that I am still here. I am still standing right next to all my children.

I cry every Mother's Day. I cry because of the best blessing of my life and now that I am a mother, I cannot imagine the pain of being without my children, no matter the circumstances, no matter the decisions. It must be so heartbreaking to not be able to raise your children.

I have dedicated my life from the day they were born to love, protect and nurture them. They are a piece of me. They chose me.

It seems I also chose my mother, but I was hell-bent on changing the course of history. I was going to do better. I was going to do the best I possibly could. I was never going to leave their sight.

I cry at every birthday, because for me that symbolises another year of successful parenting, successful mothering. For me, being present in their lives is the best gift I could have ever given myself.

I have never had any affection as a child, and I have never had a parent tell me they love me; I have never known the love of a parent.

I can assure you my children never have to wonder. Every moment of my life is about more than just telling them I love them. It is about also showing them.

Sometimes, the love is tough, but it is love. I adore them; they are such wonderful little people all sent to hug my heart.

We have a hectic household, as you would imagine. My husband is also a successful entrepreneur, but we share the load and we are there for the kids. We prioritise them. When I am travelling, he is the parent in charge and so am I when he is away. We share raising them equally.

I will always hold dear the special bond we share in raising our family. He helped me a great deal in becoming the woman that I am today. He helps me with the gaps that I have when it comes to family, but it is never an obvious thing; only I know that it is a gap. We have found a rhythm and we complement one another very well.

Believe or not, he is the disciplinarian. I am a marshmallow of a mother, but I have very clear boundaries and discipline must be upheld. I believe in conscious parenting and I always treat my children with the respect they deserve. I believe you get back what you put into them.

We are blessed with children with wonderful temperaments; they are highly appreciative, have great manners, and are just absolute sweethearts. I am unashamed to say that I sometimes use his name in vain with my son, because boys are always going to push you right to the edge of the boundary. There are times when I am out of words and options, so I whip out, "I am going to tell your father" and order is immediately restored.

I was shocked the first time I uttered those words. The reaction I received made me smile, inside. So, I always go to that place when I am desperate.

I believe children do not belong to us. God gives them to us so that we can raise, nurture, and release them to the world so that they can impact other's lives and do the same in raising theirs.

They are not my possession; whilst highly entertaining, they are what I will leave behind as my legacy. The footprints they will walk in are those I would like them to be proud of. I am working on this every moment of my life.

I build lasting memories with them. I have also been granted an opportunity to re-live my own childhood; only this time I am the author of it.

The life my children enjoy is the life I would have loved as a child; happy, free, protected, and full of laughter and adventure.

We travel a great deal because I want them to be

comfortable with the world. I want them to have multiple perspectives of life. I am so blessed to have a life partner that shares in my vision and enjoys it just as much. I am always in a jovial mood because my children remind me to live just through their own reality. The best times of my life are when I am with them.

Do not misunderstand me; it does not mean things always work out the way I planned but they are never deal breakers because of my outlook on life. I approach everything with gratitude. I move on quickly from disappointments and I focus on what matters.

Very few things get me down now. If I am down, it sure is never for too long. I am stronger than any challenge. I was, for many years baked in the oven called life.

My children are my responsibility and I have taken great care and pleasure in raising them. There are sets of values and ways of living that I have instilled in them. As you can imagine, I did not have a template to work from.

I had no good benchmark in parenting, so I had to make up my own mind about what I believed was right. I deployed conscious parenting and followed my instincts. I have only wanted to create a lasting legacy for my children. I only ever want to leave behind lasting memories and the assurance that they are loved and that they are worthy of that love.

Through my own everyday actions, I build a different reality for them, brick by brick. I teach them about self-belief, persistence, decisions and consequences. I teach them about the value of money, looking after one another and giving to people in need. Some of the other key values I have taught them are:

- Honesty: The best way to encourage truthfulness in your child is to be a truthful person yourself. Children take cues from us, so it's important that I avoid any kind of deception, even seemingly innocent lies such as not telling Daddy I gave them sweets. Another way I promote the value of honesty, is to not overreact if my child lies to me or steals something. I encourage them to tell me the truth, to talk to me. I believe in opening the channels of communication. I want them to always feel comfortable talking to me no matter the discomfort they may feel. They must know I am always there for them without any judgement.

- Justice: I teach my children a sense of right and wrong as well as making amends where they have faltered. I ask them to take some action to remedy a wrong. Saying sorry is easy as it makes the noise go away, and it lets them off the hook without forcing them to think about their actions. Having a child make amends in a proactive way conveys a much stronger message. I do all I can to treat everyone fairly and a sense of responsibility for one's actions must always prevail.

- Determination: A value I appreciate and rate the most is determination. They must always try the most difficult challenge. I have taught them that there is no such thing as impossible. You persist and give it the best you have. I encourage them to fail, but to learn from the mistake and try again. They must never give up, because something is too difficult.

- Kindness and Consideration: I encourage my children to always be kind and considerate towards one another, and other people. They must be aware of how they relate to others. Hurting people's feelings is not always avoidable but once you realise you have, a genuine apology must be given and amends made. Over time, even a young child sees that words or actions can make another person smile or feel better.

- Love: The one thing that is in constant abundance in my home is love. Love for one another, patience, and support go hand in hand. My husband and I display affection towards each other and we tell the children we love them every day. We hug, kiss, and play with them on a daily basis, even when we have had tough days at work. There are countless declarations of love in my household. It is the glue that binds us all together. It is the key ingredient. I can practically guarantee you that the more you say "I love you" to your child, the more your child will say "I love you" back. The more hugs and kisses you give, the more your home will be filled with love and affection. And when our children feel free to express their love to us, we instill in them perhaps the greatest value of all.

Parting ways,
carving a new direction

Fourteen years into my corporate career, I decided it was time to go on my own. I had built up a lot of credibility. I had reached C-suite level in a large multinational.

But I now had a family. I wanted to own my time. I wanted to go out into the world and have a direct contribution towards alleviating unemployment in our country. I wanted to be involved with causes I enjoyed and chose. My body also just refused to keep taking the abuse. I had to make a change.

I loved my last corporate job. I had incredible support and amazing opportunities. I just felt that I could use my time a bit more effectively and efficiently. I became tired of sitting in endless meetings, the corporate bullying and always fighting my own system was wearing me down.

These were all things I once found to be exciting challenges, but my heart was no longer in it. I wanted to be present in my children's lives and play an active role. I grew tired and ashamed of being a spectator in their lives. How was I any different to my own parents?

I made the decision to leave, and I followed it through with actions. I registered my company and I subsequently resigned to run it seven months later.

Many people ask me how I did that. They ask me how I left such a plump job that carried so much power and status for entrepreneurship. *Why would you want to suffer so much and put your family at risk*, was their question?

I found this very amusing, because we have been conditioned to believe that you are protected in a corporate job. We think there is far less risk. I told them that, in fact, the higher you go in any organisation, the riskier it is for you.

I reminded them of the many corporates – some of which I worked for – that retrenched people. This has become common practice due to all the meltdowns we have had in the economy, both locally and globally.

I explained the difference in owning and running my business is that I am in charge of my own destiny. I am not at anyone's mercy. It is my time and I decide what to do with it. My success is directly correlated to my effort; somebody else and their mood do not determine it.

If you want to talk about risk, let us talk about that. I was fortunate enough to work with a caring and wonderful boss who gave me the space to grow and supported me in every way. It was just time for me to change my lifestyle.

Now, of course, not everyone is meant to be in business or be an entrepreneur. There are people who are corporate citizens through-and-through and that is more than all right. I had an amazing time as a corporate executive; it was just time for me to pursue my own interests.

I did not procrastinate, I decided, planned and executed.

I was clear about the life I wanted to live. I wanted a career that could support my life and not take away consistently. I wanted to feel happy; I wanted to have time to think.

I longed to go watch my children play soccer, do ballet, and be present for their assembly recitals. I just wanted to give myself a better chance at parenthood. I needed to give them what they rightfully deserved – my attention.

I was always into entrepreneurship, so I guess it was just a matter of time before I went into it full time and full scale.

I had my first business when I was just twenty-three. I have owned a floral business, making flower arrangement for corporates and functions. This was a very stressful business. I lost my love for flowers when I worked with them everyday. I hated the smell and I just grew tired of the logistics. I had to be at the flower market every morning at five. I would then make the orders and prepare to go deliver them and arrive at my job all before eight in the morning.

My weekends were consumed by the business. I learnt a lot, but had to shut it down.

I also sold shoes and handbags. I had a hair salon for many years, which I handed over to one of the employees after seven years. I had opened that one specifically to create a job opportunity for my sister and others.

I grew a great sense of independence when I was younger. I always told myself that only I was responsible for my life and I was willing to put in the hard work to make my dreams a reality. That work ethic did not only stand me in good stead but it also unlocked many opportunities. I never had a sense of entitlement. I believe in working for what I desire.

A taste of depression

When I met my husband, he told me of his plan to move to Cape Town. I was very clear that this was not my desire whatsoever, however, if the relationship evolved into something more serious, then this would be considered. I would support his dream.

It was not long before my commitment was tested.

We got married and moved immediately. We had already bought a house with stunning views in Hout Bay on Baviaanskloof Road, by the time the girls were born.

Life in the fair Cape was challenging. I just struggled to settle. It was harsh, cold, and strange.

I soon left my corporate job and opened a fast food franchise business in the nearby Noordhoek. I also opened a linen store in our neighborhood. Life was about to become a whole lot more interesting.

Firstly, being a black person owning businesses in Cape Town was tricky in 2008. There were just so many dynamics, but most people just thought I worked at the linen store. They did not conceive the idea that I could be the owner. It worked fine for the business and

I.

The other business was coming along okay until the massive power outages and load shedding hit us. Most of the time, we did not work, and the business relied on power. The mall did not have a generator. Another big challenge was being a young, black woman owning a business in a predominantly white and coloured area. No one wanted to support me. It was a harsh reality. Some of them would in fact tell me that I would not succeed because they did not want me there. Of all the many things I had suffered in my life, racism was one I had not encountered so brutally. Even then I carved this out as an isolated incident and did not want to paint everyone with the same brush.

The business was not halaal certified, which meant the exclusion of a few other customers as well. This was a rookie mistake on my part, as this should have factored into my research.

My franchisor did not pick this up either. I had a useless franchisor that only wanted his royalties and would not bother to support me.

So, I was hit by multiple challenges. All the time, I had twin girls under a year old and a husband who was busy with work and his MBA. It was a lot to deal with, but at twenty-nine going on thirty, I was at the height of my optimism.

I soon found myself unhappy with life in Cape Town. My businesses were not doing well at all, especially the franchise. I took the decision of closing it down, sadly, also putting a few young people out of work. I lost a lot of money in that business. It was my first attempt at big business, and it was an epic fail.

I did not fail though.

Trying to wind down that business was extremely stressful. The landlord held me to the duration of the lease. At forty thousand rands a month with costs, I was only just six months into a three-year lease. I was in deep trouble. I am not counting the cash I had convinced my husband we should use to fund the business, our own money.

I went into a situational depression. I felt guilty and ashamed for letting him down. We had a young family, just moved into a new city, and I felt responsible for drowning an enormous amount of money into this venture. For the first time in my life I felt I had put my family at risk. I am an entrepreneur through and through so I had to find some optimism and a silver lining.

Our relationship took a bit of strain. I was not in a good state and we were both trying to settle into the first year of our marriage, with two babies and two businesses, and his studies. It felt as though this was too much, even for me.

I hustled very hard to escape from the lease, but the landlord did not want to hear it. Even the franchisor wanted his marketing costs and royalties at a time when

I was closing the business.

I sent them a scathing letter, which they never even responded to. I am not talking about a fly-by-night franchisor. They were reputable in the Johannesburg market. Time and again, I would email them and phone them asking for help, but they never bothered. I was in the middle of the ocean all by myself with sharks surrounding me, and I had to swim to shore.

I did what I have always done. I believed that I would get out of this even though I was gripped in anxiety and shame, but I had to dig deep. It was not enough that I was still dealing with the trauma of my childhood; I felt I had messed up and this time, dragging my husband and my children along with. This broke my heart and I sank further into a dark place but I had to dig myself out of the hole. I had to find some strength to keep fighting. I was not going to give up.

In an article titled *How to Overcome the Shame of Failure* published recently by Joseph Steinberg, CEO of SecureMySocial, he relates a discussion he had with business coach, Silvia Christmann on how you can prevent shame from overtaking you. Silvia summarised a simple four-step process:

- Notice that you are starting to let shame rule your emotions. Become aware of your behavior and physiological responses.
- Pause and breathe. Learn how to stop, and

observe your conscious and subconscious responses, whenever shame starts to "take over" – but do so without judging yourself. Take deep breaths. Be kind to yourself the same way you would have compassion on someone else going through a difficult situation. Notice when you are avoiding getting together with people, when you are "checking out" getting defensive, or feel your heart rate going up.

- Observe your mindset. Pay attention to what you are thinking – especially to any limiting beliefs such as that you are not capable or worthy of doing something, or that you will always fail. Our minds seek confirmation of our beliefs – if you think you are unworthy you will consciously or subconsciously look for proof of that notion, which can sabotage your moving forward.

- Analyze and act. Reflect on your thoughts, and especially on what triggered the feelings of shame. Evaluate how you can see the elements contributing to the shame in a different light. Often your own perspective will be far more critical of yourself than will be the perspectives of others. With that in mind, change your attitude to one of embracing and learning from failure along the path of success, rather than viewing failure as a dead end.

I focused on trying to sell off some of the equipment in the shop to raise some funds. I emptied every single source of cash I had which meant huge credit card debt and no savings. The franchisor did not even offer or accept my proposal for them to buy back the equipment and furnishings. They could have used it for another store. It was barely six months old. They ignored me and never even said goodbye.

I kept my head down and pushed to negotiate terms with the landlord. We agreed that I pay off the debt over a couple of months. That was hard. I could not bear to face my husband but I had to. I decided I was going to find the lesson in this experience.

Darrah Brustein, Founder of *Equitable Payments, Network Under/Over 40, and Finance Whiz Kids* writes that today's current fifty percent divorce rate is evidence enough that marriage is challenging. But, what if you impose an extra challenge on top of that? How does having one or both partners be entrepreneurs impact the likelihood for marital success?

She spoke with Trisha Harp, founder of the *Harp Family Institute (HFI)*, who's focus is on the impact that entrepreneurship has on relationships and, inversely, the impact relationships have on businesses.

Harp has dedicated her career to studying the effects of entrepreneurship on relationships, and she is no stranger to the topic herself. She is the daughter of an entrepreneurial marriage and is married to an entrepreneur. After continually hearing terms such as "entrepreneur's widow" as well as stories about the overwhelming failure rates for entrepreneurial marriages, Harp chose to write her master's thesis on "Spousal Satisfaction in Entrepreneurial Couples."

En route, one thing that stood out, she says, is how "many entrepreneurial researchers reported how vital the spouse/support network was in an entrepreneur's life, but [how] little data had actually been collected to determine just *how* important."

Now in her post-graduate phase, Harp has spent the last decade gathering data and interviewing hundreds of entrepreneurs and their spouses, to learn "as much as I can about the best practices of the most satisfied couples."

Overall, she says, her data has confirmed that when entrepreneurial couples—couples with at least one entrepreneur in the household—follow a few key steps, their relationships, though challenging because of the business, are not doomed. Here are her top six findings that may give hope for entrepreneurial relationships:

1. In spite of the odds, most spouses would marry their entrepreneur again. "Our research shows that eighty seven percent of respondents have experienced cash flow problems at some point in time with their company," Harp says. And during those cash-flow problems, entrepreneurs reported, their sex lives decreased, she shared. It has been well documented that

the top two reasons for divorce are money and sex. So, why does the data indicate that when spouses were asked: "Knowing what you know now about being the spouse of an entrepreneur, would you still marry your entrepreneur?" eighty eight percent said yes?

"One reason," Harp explains, "is that, in spite of the roller-coaster ride that defines entrepreneurship, spouses have reported a great feeling that they are 'on this journey together.' There is a strong desire to stick it out. HFI data also shows that when couples create a shared vision for their future, their satisfaction in all areas of life increases."

2. Creating shared business and family goals leads directly to greater happiness. Harp's data showed that entrepreneurs who set shared long-term business and family goals with their spouses scored higher in every area of satisfaction than those who didn't. On her surveys, entrepreneurs who set shared business goals were seventeen percent happier than those who didn't; and twenty seven percent who set shared family goals reported higher levels of satisfaction. Of those who set shared family goals, ninety eight percent reported being still in love with their spouse.

3. Positive outcomes result from sharing the good, the bad and the ugly about the business. Contrary to what one might believe, Harp's data showed that when entrepreneurs shared both positive and negative aspects of the business on a regular basis, the other spouse's

trust and confidence in the entrepreneur actually increased. "Sharing on a regular basis increases the spouse's belief in their entrepreneur's ability to succeed," Harp says.

"When the entrepreneur chooses not to share, the spouse usually knows when something is wrong, simply by observing his/her partner's demeanor. The not knowing leads to frustration, anxiety and impatience," Harp says. However, when the entrepreneur shares on a regular basis, "the spouse is privy to the solutions the entrepreneur is considering," she adds.

And discussions make the non-entrepreneur spouse feel as if he or she is contributing. "This helps increase a spouse's 'buy-in' and makes them feel as if it is 'our' company instead of just 'your company,'" Harp says.

4. Entrepreneurs and spouses need to be on the same team. As the saying goes, it's lonely at the top. When an entrepreneur comes home, he or she comes back to a partner, not an employee. "When a couple feels as though they are in this together, it supports both members of the team. It's 'us versus them,'.

When spouses on Harp's surveys were asked how they handled stressful financial challenges, their number one answer was, "We supported each other fully," she says. Now, of course, it's up to both the entrepreneur and the spouse to determine how that support plays out, "but, asking pointed questions such as, "When you're stressed out because of the business, what can I do to make you feel supported?' is always a good idea," Harp says.

5. Entrepreneurs genuinely appreciate their spouses. Her data also confirmed that entrepreneurs actually have a significant level of gratitude for everything their spouses do for them. The problem, however, is that spouses don't realise their that entrepreneur-partners believe they [the spouses] are important to the success of the company.

"Directly showing your appreciation is one way to ensure you both know how meaningful your role is to the family, the business and each other," Harp advises. "Grab a stack of Post-Its and write a bunch of love notes on them. Be sure to include ways they help with all aspects of your life, including family and business. During dinner, be sure to thank your partner for something very specific they did to make your life a little easier."

6. It's important to be loving, fun, intelligent and honest.

Harp looked at how entrepreneurs and spouses characterised one another's personality characteristics. Of the top six characteristics for each, four showed up on both lists. Despite a list of roughly fifty characteristics to choose from, both individuals repeatedly chose "loving, fun, intelligent and honest".

"It's been written that people often choose partners who complement us and fill our holes," Harp says.

"Entrepreneurs choose partners who can keep up with them, emotionally and intellectually. That's a pretty solid foundation for any marriage!"

I identify with all of the above. You may be in for some rocky times, but, as Harp advises, as long as you set shared goals, communicate often, directly appreciate one another, and continue to respect each other's contributions, entrepreneurial couples can rise above the challenge, letting you live happily ever after.

I remember telling him that I think we are being prepared for a future of abundance, but we needed this experience early on in our marriage. Little did I know that he would also become an entrepreneur and I would be his pillar in times when he desperately needed me to be.

I said to him that I knew without a shadow of doubt that we were going to be okay, but we first, needed to cement our union and ground it through this hardship. It is very difficult to stay positive in the middle of a trying time. I had so much to think about, handle, and pull it all together. I had to stand firm and strong, not just for me, but also for him.

I felt he had a right to be angry and disappointed. He told me to obtain funding, but I convinced him otherwise, and I believed the business would be able to pay us back. Honestly, I would make the same decision again if it meant protecting our primary asset, our home. I grew a little wiser of course, and I now know how to fund businesses, but nothing is ever fail-proof, otherwise everyone would be doing it.

I was still standing, so I went back to the corporate world. I needed to work to be able to pay back all the debt I had accrued. I never missed my payments and I just kept grinding myself out of the hole. It took a long time before I could get out of that and start to breathe a little. It took years, but I never doubted my ability to rise again.

I made another crucial decision. When we moved to Cape Town, my husband made me a promise that if I did not like it, we would go back home, no questions asked. So, eighteen months into our stint in the new city, we moved back home, Johannesburg a place of dreams.

I have always loved the energy in Johannesburg. As different and diverse as we are, it always felt as though we were headed in the same direction. I stuck out like a sore thumb in Cape Town. I hated living there, compounded by my business troubles. It felt so great to be back. My husband never argued with me when I said I wanted to go home. I needed the emotional support of a familiar place with familiar people. I needed to feel energised again. It turned out he also felt the same.

I stayed out of the business lane for a number of years as I recovered from that burn. I was bruised and battered but I knew that it was a life I was always going to go back to.

The thrill of risk and reward has always driven me. I always ask myself, what is the worst that could happen? Of course, I have had that experience, but that should never stop you from pursuing your dreams. I tell people that getting out of bed is risky; but staying in bed is just as risky, so get up and live!

I built myself up and my corporate career blossomed. I was really enjoying myself and loving the space I was in. I was part of a community. I felt alive. My relationship with my husband had recovered that terrible ordeal, but the hang-ups endured; it was rough going for a while but we had something stronger keeping us together.

We were also growing up. We decided that having one another was the only thing that mattered. In that entire time, not once did we ever talk divorce. We have never looked back since. Our union has grown and there is nothing more special that sharing in successes we both worked hard for. We delight in raising our children together and building a warm home that they know they can always come back to, no matter the winds in their own lives.

The day-bed

I am constantly in awe of the many surprises life dishes out when we least expect them.

A few years after nurturing the trees back to life in our newly acquired home in Johannesburg, I was moved to tears when I saw my old friend, the Pearl Acacia. There she was, donning bright yellow flowers as I stepped right outside my front door. She is still the only tree that sparkles with colour in the middle of a grey season.

I told my husband about that tree. I shared with my children the meaning of that tree and how it became my friend. It was such a pleasant co-incidence that the tree was in full view, no matter where I am in the house. It is so humbling for me. We remodeled the house to have large windows and doors that let nature come straight in. It was this tree that I wanted to always have full sight of.

No matter the day I have had, the tree reminds me that seasons do change. Whether I am celebrating a success, or dealing with disappointment, it is there to remind me to remain humble and grounded. I see myself under that tree all those years as a child, plotting and wishing for a great future. I had time to think.

I was a mess when my husband surprised me with a life size day-bed right under the tree. He said I could now relax under the tree, and I enjoy a glass of champagne. I count my blessings, as I take in the full view of our beautiful home and I now pick on the seeds with the children. This time, they fall onto beautiful grey and bright yellow outdoor fabric. They are easier to pick and eat. I felt like the luckiest girl in the world.

This has become a tradition in my house and the children love it when I tell them the stories of that tree. They never seem to tire of them. Reminders are all around me, and I am just so grateful for the life I have been able to build. I belong here with my family. I never doubt or daydream about what could have been, because my life is a dream come true.

Throwing in the towel is very easy. There were many times when I questioned if my life was worth living. It is through the cracks that I believe the light shines even better as it forces its way through the darkness. Battle scars truly give flavor to our character. It takes an enormous amount of investment, courage and bravery to break free from the chains of a painful past. It can be done; I am proof that your past should not be a determining factor in your future except only to teach the valuable lessons. Your pain may just be the fuel you need to push on and live a fulfilling life packed with purpose.

Hope exists; never lose heart. Keep focused on the goals and work tirelessly to see your dreams come true. Avoid distractions and only surround yourself with people who will motivate and encourage you in times when you want to give up. I want to continue being a living example that ordinary people do live extra ordinary lives.

The roaring forties

The years leading to forty had brought about their own drama. I remember three years before I turned forty, for the first time in my life, my mother asked me to go join a family lunch in KwaZulu Natal. We were in the area for December holidays, so I was okay to go. This was a lunch with her cousin with whom she had re-connected recently.

It was lovely to meet some of her family members for the first time. My brother and my sister were also present. Of course, it was the usual scrutiny from the elders, who were intrigued to see my family and me for the first time. It was sweet and uncomfortable, but necessary.

One of the elderly gentlemen told me that it was very pleasing to have spent the last two weeks with my brother. I was surprised, because I thought he had just arrived. It was bizarre. Anyway, I did not think much of it until much later as we were making our way back to Johannesburg.

My mother had caught a lift with us. We stopped by to check the car and make sure all was in order before we got on the road. So, I went off to have something to drink with her and my little guy. Out of the blue, I asked her what that elderly gentleman meant that my brother had been there for two weeks. I was really just asking to fill the spaces. I was never ready for the response.

At thirty-seven years old, I find out that my brother belongs to another family, that he is my half-brother. Naturally, this never would have mattered in my life. He was my brother. I was just so shocked and scared that my tummy just started running.

Turned out he had spent the two weeks with his real family. I could not ask any further questions, except why she would keep this from us all our lives. She was afraid we would hate him, she said.

Well, the irony of my life. I do not know if this is something they both always knew or if it was a surprise to him as well. That is his journey, I guess.

I begged my mother to please let all the skeletons out of the closet because the opportunity was there. She said she was also thinking of taking us to our family. I assured her that was not necessary for me. There was a time when this would have been the best news to hear, I was almost forty with my own family. I no longer needed that.

Of course, the older we become, the more we try to mend our ways, but I cannot take part in that. I have had enough drama; I have worked so hard to have the life that I have that I just want to focus on that and keep the energy clean.

Three months before I turned forty, I experienced a complete meltdown. In a moment, I sent my mother a very long letter detailing how I felt about all the things that happened to me, the role she played in both my childhood and the state of affairs with my brother. For the first time in my life, I poured my heart out to her. I may have vomited forty-year-old issues on her, but the force was too large for me not to say something to her. This was random, very random.

I felt I needed to clear the path to forty. The gist of the letter was that what happened to me, was not okay; that I still cry about it. I told her the pain will never go away but over the years, I had worked very hard to be a better person and to learn to live with the pain. I told her wounds like that do not heal; you just learn to keep a pile of plasters handy so that when the wound bleeds, you have something to patch it with.

I have never been that vulnerable in my life. I just wanted her to know how I really felt and yes, it may have taken me all these years to do it, but there it was. Her response to me left me cold with sleepless nights.

I felt as if I was trapped in a nightmare, but I was wide-awake. In every situation in my life, I look at my role in it first. I wondered what I had written that made her respond to me in that way. I was shaking and terrified. I wanted to go back read what I had written, but I was too scared to read it.

I have never involved my husband in some of my challenges with family. I never wanted him to take any side, because it was always going to mine. This would have had an even more negative impact, so I kept some things to myself over the years and tried to ignore, deal, or anticipate. This time, I could not hide the pain. I was not myself. I have never felt like that in my life and God, I hope I never do – ever again. Every time I tried to tell him I would just break down and cry.

Five days later, I built up the courage to read the letter again. Right then I decided if my child had written me a letter like that, the first thing I would have said is "I am sorry, I did not know you felt like that". The next thing I would have said is "How can I make it up to you, how can I take the pain away"?

One of the psychologists I have been working with recently said to me, "You know you need to face up to the fact that your mother is never going to be the mother you hope for".

He told me that I approach everything from a child expecting a mother to be a mother. I want her to think like a mother, I want her to act like one. I needed her to own up to her mistakes. I was desperate for her to just tell me she was sorry. That is all I needed, that is all I have ever needed. I just wanted her to say she was sorry.

She attacked me in a way I have never been attacked before. She blamed everybody including me, but never her. She spoke of how she was now so happy to finally learn about the reasons why I hated her so much.

She told me the young guy who killed his older brother still happily lives with his mom. What did I expect her to do? Kill my brother so that I could feel better? This was in response to me asking her to stop bringing my brother to my house as I am sacred of him and I do not feel comfortable having him in my house. I just asked her to stop forcing him down my throat. I found it disrespectful to my family and me. That day, she essentially told me once again that my life was not as important as my brother's.

Anyway, there is so much that was said on that day. I came out of that a whole different person. I, for the first time in my life, realised that truly, my mother does not know how to be a mother even when it is staring her in the face. I realised that there is absolutely nothing there. I kept knocking on the door and no one was home. I once again had to embrace a very crude truth.

The psychologist was correct in every way, I had just been hoping and hanging onto something that was never there and would never be a reality. The truth hurt so much, but it was liberating.

So much hurt was directed towards me. After I got over the initial shock, I started feeling sorry for my mother. I realised that she really needs to forgive herself.

The reality of my situation culminated in that moment. My mother has never had the ability to be a mother. She further made choices that did not enable her to be a mother. Everything is about her and it was not going to change.

It was at this moment that I truly had a breakthrough. I spoke to the child inside me and told her "Let her go, just let her go". I sobbed uncontrollably, but for the first time in my life, I mourned the loss of my mother.

I lost my mother the day she left me. She was never there and she never was going to be there. I decided in that moment to stop having expectations of her. I ceased to wish she could just be kind to me. I ended all hopes that she would just love me.

I felt liberated when I came to this realisation. It still does not take the pain away. I have just accepted that there are things I cannot change. I guess I chose her to be my mother because of what I needed to break the cycle. God had facilitated this process of growth in me.

I finally realised that all the work I had done over my entire life to become a better person, to keep bitterness at bay – she never got to do all that work. Our circumstances may have been different, but the outcome was the same. She had no mother and no father to raise her.

I have been looking for something from her that she was not capable of giving to me because she herself still needed to come to terms with her own childhood, her own situation.

She has recently been opening up more. I am not sure if it is old age looming, but she is reaching out a whole lot more. She is – for the first time – owning up to her mistakes and taking responsibility for her decisions. She still has to work on herself and there is no expiry date on that. That, however, is her journey.

I knew early on that I needed to work on myself; I had foresight that I had to change the script, but that would take work – lots of it. I am in no way perfect; far from it. I am still a work in progress for as long as I shall live. Who knows what is beyond the grave? Maybe I will still be working on myself even then. Nothing has ever come easy to me.

It took until I was forty for my mother to tell me she was sorry. That last engagement we had and her response may have gotten her thinking, but not before an amazing display of drama. The apology came with all sorts of 'other people blame', but, it was the first apology I had ever received from her. I told her I accepted it.

In fact, I forgave her many years ago, but the little girl inside me needed to hear her say she was sorry. The child in us never goes away; we just learn to pacify that child – at times completely to our detriment. As adults we learn skills and equip ourselves with tools and techniques to deal with the inner child. Some do it successfully, others not so much. But the bottom line is the same; the pain never goes away. You just learn to live with it.

No matter what, she is my mother. Our relationship is still very fragile. It is honestly not because of lack of trying. So much gets in the way and it is just a constant struggle to relate.

Oprah Winfrey wrote on her website that forgiving our parents is a core task of adulthood, and one of the most crucial kinds of forgiveness. We see our parents in our mates, in our friends, in our bosses, even in our children. When we have felt rejected by a parent and have remained in that state, we will inevitably feel rejected by these important others as well. But letting our parents off the hook, psychologist Robert Karen says, is the first step toward happiness, self-acceptance and maturity.

Oprah further advocates the steps below to help the healing begin:

- Resolve resentment: Nursing resentments toward a parent does more than keep that parent in the doghouse. We become stuck there, too, forever the child, the victim, the have-not in the realm of love. Strange as it may seem, a grudge is a kind of clinging, a way of not separating, and when we hold a grudge against a parent, we are clinging not just to the parent, but more specifically to the bad part of the parent. It's as if we don't want to live our lives until we have this resolved and feel the security of their unconditional love. We do so for good reasons psychologically. But the result is just the opposite: We stay locked into the badness and we don't grow up.

- Develop realistic expectations: The sins of parents are among the most difficult to forgive. We expect the world of them, and we do not wish to lower our expectations. Decade after decade, we hold out the hope, often unconsciously, that they will finally do right by us. We want them to own up to all their misdeeds, to apologize, to make heartfelt pleas for our forgiveness. We want our parents to embrace us, to tell us they know we were good children, to undo the favoritism they've shown to a brother or sister, to take back their hurtful criticisms, to give us their praise.

- Hold on to the good: Most parents love their children, with surprisingly few exceptions. But no parent is perfect—which means that everyone has childhood wounds. If we're lucky, our parents were good enough for us to be able to hold on to the knowledge of their love for us and our love for them, even in the face of the things they did that hurt us.

- Foster true separation: To forgive is not to condone the bad things our parents have done. It's not to deny their selfishness, their rejections, their meanness, their brutality, or any of the other misdeeds, character flaws, or limitations that may attach to them. It is important to separate from our parents—which is to stop seeing ourselves as children who depend on them for our emotional well-being, to stop being their victims, to recognize that we are adults with some capacity to shape our own lives and the responsibility to do so.

- Let your parents back into your heart: When we do that, we can begin to understand the circumstances and limitations they labored under, recognize the goodness in them that our pain has pushed aside, feel some compassion perhaps, not only for the hard journey they had but also for the pain we have caused them.

- Commit to the journey: Getting to a forgiving place, finding the forgiving self inside us, is a long and complicated journey. We have to be ready to forgive. We have to want to forgive. The deeper the wound, the more difficult the process—which makes forgiving parents especially hard. Along the way, we may have to

> express our protest, we may have to be angry
> and resentful, we may even have to punish our
> parents by holding a grudge. But when we
> arrive there, the forgiveness we achieve will be
> forgiveness worth having.

I am nowhere near the levels she refers to. I have been able to achieve some things on this journey, but have failed dismally in others. Honestly, I simply have no interest or energy to tackle some. There is a whole lot that I have to deal with. I have prioritised that which I needed to reach a mental state that allows me to live a fulfilled life. I have also learnt to be patient with myself and not work according to other people's clocks. I listen to my own rhythm. I feel empty every time I try. The hurt continues in many different forms. Often I just keep to myself and guard my soul, perhaps I am too guarded when it comes to her. I am still working on this. It is incredibly difficult to give a parent something they never put in you to begin with. The little girl in me shows up in all my engagements with my mother. I am now at a place where I …

I respect my mother both as the person who gave me life and as an elder. She will never go to bed on an empty stomach. I will always look after her needs as much as I can. She will always have access to my house and my children, her grandchildren. My mother gave me the best gift of all; she gave birth to me. I salute her and honor her for that.

Forgiving does not mean forgetting. The facts of my childhood are the facts. I will always be cut up about it, but it no longer controls me. Some nights I cry about it, other days I do not even think about it. It will always be a part of me. It has enabled me to be the person that I am today, to care about the things I care about. I pray that someday, my mother forgives herself and accept things she cannot change.

In Awaken the Giant Within, Anthony Robbins says, "Instead of just conditioning yourself to feel differently about rejection and eliminating fearful behaviors, you can adopt a new global belief that says 'I am the source of all my emotions. Nothing and no one can change how I feel except me'.

This has been a challenge, but one I have tackled with great enthusiasm.

Cancer. Really?

I can tell you that my fortieth year arrived with a bang. She did not knock politely and ask to have a seat in my house. In the months leading up to my birthday, I had a very serious health scare.

I have always been very diligent with my annual check-ups. I would not miss a pap smear and I would do my blood screenings. For the last couple of years, my pap smears have returned abnormal results. They were very inconsistent, but the abnormal cells would go away by the next pap smear.

Starting in 2016, the abnormal cells just kept coming back. I went into surgery late 2016 to have them removed. My gynaecologist did a colposcopy LLETZ (long loop excision of the transformation zone of the cervix). They conducted more tests on the tissue sample they had cut, and it showed that the abnormalities had been removed successfully.

I had my annual pap smear again in 2017, and this time the abnormal cells had returned. My gynaecologist and I had a serious discussion about it. She kept assuring me that I do not have cervix cancer, but that these were just cells that kept coming back and we needed to deal with them once and for all. She knew we did not want any more children, but she had to check again that status quo remained.

She told me I had a couple of months to pick a date for the surgery. I decided to wait until I had a blast celebrating my fortieth birthday before I went back in for surgery. I had gone under four times in the last two years for various reasons, and I was afraid. I am always loath to keep knocking on that door, in case someone might answer.

In March of 2018, a mere two weeks after my fortieth birthday, I went in for the surgery. I was happy that I had celebrated a significant milestone in my life and was ready for anything.

This time my doctor and I had agreed that we are not going to be conservative. We had to be aggressive in fighting this before it became a terminal matter. I said goodbye to my cervix on that day. The surgery took about an hour. I had taken an Uber there. I was discharged later that afternoon, caught an Uber, and went home. No big deal but it was a big deal. I just carried on with life.

I have since made a good recovery and the tests came back satisfactory. I may be at a lesser risk now, but I will never be completely out of the woods. I am just glad that I was diligent with my screenings; otherwise, I could have found myself with a serious case of cervix cancer. It is a treatable cancer but yet, thousands of women die from it every year due to missed pap smears.

A time also came for me to have my very first mammogram. Forty sure brings a lot of administration. I was nervous but optimistically confident. I was praying for a positive outcome.

When the doctor was done, everything was clear, except that I had enlarged lymph nodes and although she was not worried because the breasts themselves were clear, she needed me to come back in another two weeks to re-do the scan just so she could be one hundred percent sure. I was battling a cold at the time, and she said it is possible that they were enlarged because my body was trying to fight off the infection. Okay, not really the news I wanted to hear but I was still optimistic.

I went straight to Dr. Google and I was mortified to read that the lymph nodes in the under arm are the first areas breast cancer is likely to spread to. I thought she just did not want to worry me, but the truth is that I had early stages of breast cancer. I worried myself sick for about a week and I decided to snap out of it. I would beat this like I had beaten everything else in my life.

I went back as scheduled, only to find the nodes had not shrunk back to normal size. Okay, again not the outcome I had hoped for. Now I was convinced that I had breast cancer, but still remained hopeful. She had to do a lymph node biopsy to remove tissue for observation and further testing.

I love how doctors tell you a procedure is going to be very quick with very little to no pain. *All you will feel is a prick.*

The procedure took about thirty minutes, and it was excruciating. She had to draw two samples. I complained bitterly at the huge needle she was using and for lying to me about the pain.

Again, I had to wait for a few days for the results. It is very difficult to concentrate on anything else when you are waiting for what could be life-changing results. I tried to fill the days but I could not even sleep. My mind was racing and I was sure that there is no way I can dodge another bullet again.

Finally, the results came back and there were no signs of breast cancer. I was okay once again, so onto the next screening then.

I am grateful for my health as without it, none of what I do is even possible. It was a crippling reminder of the things we do tend to take for granted. I was so pleased that my health has never been one of those things I take for granted, I have always been diligent in order to give myself a chance.

The tragic and sudden loss of my best friend and my business mentor – two very significant people in my life – also became part of my DNA as I turned forty. Within three months, I had lost them both.

Coping with the loss of someone you love is one of life's biggest challenges. Often, the pain of loss can feel overwhelming. I experienced all kinds of difficult and unexpected emotions; from shock and anger to disbelief, guilt, and profound sadness. The pain of grief can also disrupt your physical health, making it difficult to sleep, eat, or even think straight. I am still working through the grief and can only now remember the fond memories we shared together. I miss their presence very much. Life is not the same without them, but I am still standing and I soldier on. So, I walked into forty with a heavy heart, but a grateful soul.

Conclusion

I have experienced immeasurable success in my personal life and my career. I have made peace with my childhood. I have forgiven all there is to forgive.

God has blessed me with a wonderful husband and three beautiful children who love me unconditionally. They give me a place where I belong, a home. I have learned from my mother's mistakes. I do all I have to in order for my children to be safe and have a loving home. I have more information at my disposal, along with strong instincts and an undying desire to have positively contributed to their lives.

I pray every day that I am able to change the course of history through my own actions and the opportunities I give to my children. They have a good relationship with their grandmother.

I still do not know my father. I no longer have a need to. I have made peace with that. That will always be my reality, even if I met him some day. He never existed as far as I'm concerned.

Through my roles in the corporate world and my career as an entrepreneur, I have been afforded an opportunity to make a difference in people's lives. I contribute to their betterment. I do this every day. I am a mentor. I relish the opportunity to give back through some of the lessons I have learned in life.

I share myself and my time with people who are lost, confused, and at times have no hope. I believe in giving more than just money back to struggling communities. I have worked with some amazing people to drive charitable initiatives. My businesses afford me the platform to grow other businesses, especially women-owned businesses. I feel alive when I am helping others realise their dreams.

I have been doing a lot of talks in corporates and other platforms where people hear my story and feel encouraged. They walk away hopeful; that no matter what their circumstances, they have a chance.

It does not matter where you have come from, it matters what you do with your life from there on. There truly is nothing impossible when you set your mind to it. If you believe you can, then you will.

The opposite is also true, so you decide which side of the fence you will be on and which side you would like history to judge you by.

I have received amazing recognition for my work. The many awards and the recognition on multiple platforms are testament to reaping the rewards of hard work.

People are always tempted to think and believe that

I got lucky along the way. I am telling my story so that I can share with people that luck can only take you so far. Something inside you must drive the direction you want your life to take.

Luck is not sustainable. Dreams do not come true until you start working to achieve your goals. The dream life is now. There is no other life reserved somewhere for us to start living. Let us make this life the dream we always wanted to come true.

Work for it and the rewards will come. Be patient, humble, and persistent in your approach. Be very clear about the vision you want for your life and do everything in your power to enable that.

Spend time understanding, that which enables and that which disables your dreams. Use your energy only on the things that will fulfill your purpose.

I live a life full of purpose; I am a living example of self-belief; hard work; perseverance, and optimism. I am not done yet.

Opportunities come my way not because of luck, but because I have built the foundation brick by brick so that I can exploit the opportunity the moment I see it. So many have opportunities land on their lap, but they cannot even recognise them. They have no eyes to see.

I create my own opportunities through focused hard work and the positive energy I put out there. I have amazing relationships that I treasure, especially in business.

I am not lucky; I possess a distinct work ethic and I can never stay down. I have learnt to embrace my pain and myself. I have found something even more special inside me as I have grown. I need that child inside me to stay, because she is a great reminder of what it has taken for me to reach this point. I love myself with all the cracks and flaws. I am immensely proud of the work I have put into my life.

I recently returned from being celebrated in France. Winning the prestigious Veuve Clicquot ELLE boss award was one of the best highlights of my life. This award honours inspiring businesswomen who empower, support and encourage female creativity and leadership.

I was hosted in Reims, along with nine other women from other countries around the world. It was an epic time that culminated with a vine named after me in Verzy, one of Veuve Clicquot's villages in the champagne valley. My very own name in the champagne valley? It is still hard to believe, and I keep looking inwards and I tell that little girl in there that she was always going to be okay. She is okay.

Having my work recognised in this manner and having these platforms opened up for me has been humbling. My own personal brand has been enhanced. People and large corporates have opened their arms and welcomed me. They have embraced my story, my purpose, and me.

I have embraced God's plan for my life over the years. I was born for the life I am living. I never feel like an imposter, this is the life I worked for. This is the life I envisioned.

I have found strength in my purpose. I have enough fuel to keep pushing on, no matter the weather. I now sit on boards of listed companies. I am a sought-after business partner. I have graced covers of many magazines. My face has beamed through the airways onto television sets, but I still remain that young girl who had to fight for everything.

My credibility has carried me through all these years, and everything is just being released to the universe. My drive built up my credibility and my belief fueled my purpose. My faith sustains my purpose. My name is highly sought out for motivation, to inspire hope in those who have none.

It is very easy to be despondent when you are in a valley, but it is in this precise moment that you are being baked for what is to come. Your mental ability to withstand challenges and push on sets you apart from the pack. I was baked in pain and came out the other side a human being who can relate at any level, one that empathises. Above all, I choose to spread kindness.

I have also learnt throughout my life that we all have a story to tell and there is always that one person listening whose life may forever be changed.

People from all walks of life have supported me, encouraged me without even knowing my background. Those that have come to know it, throw their whole weight of prayers behind me in support and at times solidarity because we are truly never alone.

My achievements and every bit of success I strive for is not only mine, it is for these people. It is for people who look at me and can identify with my struggles. I do not just represent myself; I represent a nation of believers, hopefuls, and an undying human spirit to rise above all challenges and thrive.

Everyone needs a cheerleader; someone to pick you up when you feel the world crushing down on your shoulders. I surround myself with positive people. I always seek advice and guidance from my coaches and mentors. This also keeps me grounded. My strong value system sustains me and shows me the way, every day. I continue to evolve and re-invent myself. I am of a very strong positive mind and I have amazing self-belief.

I make mistakes because I strive for excellence rather than perfection. Not everything goes according to my wishes or plans, but I have learnt to release things not meant for me. I feel saved from an unforeseen disaster when something does not go my way.

Challenges are an everyday part of my life. I choose to only see the positive and brave the negative. I do my best to feed my soul with only what is good for it. In his introduction in *Care of the Soul*, Thomas says, "When soul is neglected, it does not just go away; it appears symptomatically in obsessions, addictions, violence and loss of meaning". He says "When you look closely at the image of soulfulness, you see that it is tied to life in all its particulars – good food, satisfying conversations, genuine friends and experiences that stay in the memory and touch the heart".

He advocates for a philosophy of soulful living and techniques for dealing with everyday problems without striving for perfection or salvation. I falter sometimes, but I keep trying every day. I am not bitter; instead, I cultivated kindness. I am not sad, I am loved, and there is no greater love than the love of self.

I had the courage to keep fighting my demons and eventually learned to embrace them; they stopped attacking me the day I gave up resisting them. They sometimes rise up and pick a fight with me, and on some days, I give in, but mostly, I do not. I tell them to shut up and sit down. I have developed an amazing relationship with the little girl inside.

Bruce Barton says, "Nothing splendid has ever been achieved, except by those who dared believe that something inside of them was superior". He further says "If you have anything really valuable to contribute to the world, it will come through the expression of your own personality, that single spark of divinity that sets you off and makes you different from every other living creature."

I love the person I have become. I have embraced her with great love and kindness, knowing that she battled through some really tough situations and yet, she is still standing.

I have shown bravery in living the best possible life in spite of it all. For as long as I am still standing, I will fight for what is right, fair, and just for all those who cannot fight for themselves. I will continue to do this through giving people a chance at a dignified life, for I know what it is like to have your dignity stripped away from you every day.

I guess I agree that one's upbringing plays a role in the character they become. I also have found – through my own experience – that you must decide what role your upbringing will play and what kind of character you want to build.

As indicated earlier, there is much proven research on the effects of child abuse. The odds are stacked against survivors. When they do survive, they are faced with a mountain of burden, shame and low self-worth. Popular script says people like me, with such a traumatic childhood with clear neglect and abandonment, have low to no chance of turning their lives around. Well, I am living proof that you can. Psychologists continue to be baffled and keep asking the question "What sets people apart"? Is it nature or is it nurture?

Social Scientists alike continue to try to find the answer to this lifelong question. How can three little children who had exactly the same circumstances turn out so differently?

I have myself been involved in numerous debates about this, if not being the subject of the debate. My siblings have both turned out completely different from me and have led very different lives, most of which is not successful according to conventional description of success. I always, decisively, lean towards free will, but what does that really mean? Does it even exist?

Peter Gooding, a PhD Candidate of Psychology from the University of Essex writes; from coffee table books and social media to popular science lectures, it seems it has become increasingly fashionable for neuroscientists, philosophers, and other commentators to tell anyone that will listen that free will is a myth.

But why is this debate relevant to anyone but a philosophy student keen to impress a potential date? Actually, a growing body of evidence from Psychology suggests belief in free will matters enormously for our behaviour. It is also becoming clear that how we talk about free will affects whether we believe in it.

He says, in the lab, using deterministic arguments to undermine people's belief in free will has led to a number of negative outcomes, including increased cheating and aggression. It has also been linked to a reduction in helping behaviours and lowered feelings of gratitude.

In the conversation.com Peter Gooding further says that a recent study showed that it is possible to diminish people's belief in free will by simply making them read a science article suggesting that everything is predetermined. This made the participants' less willing to donate to charitable causes (compared to a control group). This was only observed in non-religious participants, however. Scientists argue that these outcomes may be the result of a diminished sense of agency and control that comes with believing that we are free to make choices. Similarly, we may also feel less moral responsibility for the outcomes of our actions.

He carries on saying that it may therefore be unsurprising that some studies have shown that people who believe in free will are more likely to have positive life outcomes – such as happiness, academic success and better work performance. However, the relationship between free will belief and life outcomes may be complex so this association is still debated.

A growing body of evidence has further shown that believing in free will is associated with a variety of positive life outcomes, including feeling grateful for past events (MacKenzie et al., 2014), better job performance (Stillman et al., 2010), higher academic achievement (Feldman et al., 2016), passionate love (Boudesseul et al., 2016), satisfaction with life (Li et al.,

2017), and lower levels of perceived stress (Crescioni et al., 2015).

Nonetheless, the extent to which belief in free will per se is associated with positive life outcomes or whether some third variable is driving these associations remains to be explored. One possibility is that the relationship between free will beliefs and positive life outcomes, such as satisfaction with one's life, might be confounded by a sense of personal control.

Indeed, it is well-established that a sense of personal control is positively associated with many of the same positive life outcomes that relate to free will beliefs, including subjective well-being (for reviews, see Myers and Diener, 1995; Peterson, 1999; Ross and Mirowsky, 2013). Thus, it is unclear whether these beliefs are uniquely associated with indicators of subjective well-being over and above a sense of personal control.

In their work exploring lay understandings of free will, Monroe and Malle (2010, 2014) found that people's definitions of what it means to have free will differed from philosophical understandings that typically view free will as the ability for our conscious minds (or a soul) to make decisions, regardless of brain states or prior causal events (Harris, 2012). Rather, people defined free will as their freedom to make choices and the ability to act without constraints—that is, their sense of personal control (see also Baumeister and Monroe, 2014).

This debate will rage on for many more generations and centuries to come. I say, let no one ever tell you what you should be and who you should become. I do not believe I am more special than the next human being. I made the decision to own my life, not point fingers, even with plenty opportunity.

I have never acted as if I were a victim. I recognised that I had been dealt a rotten card and it was my responsibility to work with that card and make sure that the outcome was what I desired.

I woke up one day and decided that I was not my mother's mistakes and my father's rejection. I was not the shame of the abuse. I could decide to let that define me, or I could prove that I am worthy of greatness.

I chose the latter. I cemented in my mind that I will be a living and identifiable example that it can be done. I worked on myself, endlessly and tirelessly. I knew from a very early age that it would take work to overcome my hurdles, so I went to work, only stopping to gasp some air but never lost sight of the goal, the dream life.

My extended family gave me nourishment and a roof over my head when I needed it the most, and for that I will always be grateful. The lessons I took away from my life with them were life-defining; they shaped me to be who I am today.

The role they played in my life was exactly as it was meant to be. A myriad of good came out of it. I am a soldier of life and the human spirit always triumphs, no matter the odds. If you set your mind on something, you best believe you can achieve it.

Nelson Mandela famously says "It seems impossible until it is done".

I am a work in progress, always striving for the impossible. I chuckle every time I smash a goal. I stop, take a deep breath, say a deep prayer, and carry on.

We were all born for greatness and the only thing we should fear is never realising our full potential. The only person standing between you and your dreams is yourself. I celebrate my life every day. because it is well worth the effort and it sure is worth living.

I savor every ounce of my success because I know what it has taken to achieve it. I value myself and the contribution I make to society. I have grown into the life I was meant to live; one of purpose, love, and immeasurable self-worth.

All these experiences, defining in every right have shaped me to become the person you hear about or see and experience today. The pain I was baked in shaped me to be an empathetic and kind person who constantly wants to make a positive difference in other people's lives. I know what it feels like to be in what seems like a hopeless situation. I have lived through many years of people trying to break me as a result I am overly protective of those who cannot stand up for themselves. At times it comes at huge personal cost but that is a very small matter compared to the satisfaction of lending my voice to someone who really needs it.

I have a very positive outlook on life with the amazing ability to relate to people at different levels and across the gender and colour lines. I am very passionate about my country and I thrive when I am at the forefront of eradicating poverty by creating sustainable job opportunities. I can identify a lot with the pain of the ordinary person on the street. I open up all the doors I have access to and kick down those I have none for others to have a chance at a dignified life. I remain very optimistic about South Africa. The wounds of apartheid are still very fresh. This system de-humanised our people and separated families. Above it all, it robbed us of an opportunity to get to know one another. We truly can never understand where a person comes from until we authentically listen to their story. We remain a very divided nation, but I have hope that someday we will find our way.

I spend most of my time mentoring young women and men who are going through similar journeys. It is very important for them to understand that they should never lose hope. I share with them and now the world my story so that people can see themselves in it and know that if you set your mind on the right things and the right path, then you too can be a nation builder in spite of your circumstances. It starts by understanding what those right things are and how you can go about achieving them even when the voices inside your head tell you it cannot be done.

I have only just begun, and the road ahead is long but the journey is fulfilling. The dream life is now. I was baked in pain but came out on the other side with enough mental and emotional resources to live a life of service to others.

References

1. "Mthethwa – historical state, Africa". britannica.com. Retrieved 10 April 2018.

2. Morris, Donald R. (1965). The Washing of the Spears: The Rise of the Zulu Nation under Shaka and its fall in the Zulu War of 1879. New York: Simon and Schuster. OCLC 408488., reprinted in 1998 by Da Capo Press, Cambridge, ISBN 0-306-80866-8

3. References: SAHISTORY.org

   • Homelands or the dumping grounds? (Online) available at: https://newhistory.co.za/Part-4-Chapter-14-A-state-of-change-Homelands-or-dumping-grounds/ [accessed on 10 September 2014]

   • Butler, Jeffrey, Robert I. Rotberg, and John Adams. (1978). The Blacks Homelands of South Africa: The Political and Economic Development of Bophuthatswana and Kwa-Zulu. Berkeley: University of California Press.

   • The history of the homeland history essay. (online) available at: https://www.ukessays.com/essays/history/the-history-of-the-homelands-history-essay.php [accessed on 11 September 2014]

4. https://explorable.com/nature-vs-nurture-debate-Sarah Mae Sincero

5. https://www.verywellmind.com/what-is-nature-versus-nurture-2795392

6. https://nateherbst-sociologycity.weebly.com/nature-v-nurture.html

7. https://www.goodtherapy.org/learn-about-therapy/issues/abuse

8. https://aifs.gov.au/cfca/publications/effects-child-abuse-and-neglect-adult-survivors

9. http://theconversation.com/the-psychology-of-believing-in-free-will-97193

10. https://www.frontiersin.org/articles/10.3389/fpsyg.2018.00623/full

11. https://www.entrepreneur.com/article/276449

12. https://www.havoca.org/survivors/attitudes/self-esteem/

13. https://www.psychologytoday.com/us/blog/somatic-psychology/201303/trauma-childhood-sexual-abuse

14. https://www.archmil.org/offices/sexual-abuse-prevention/stages-healing.htm

Printed in Great Britain
by Amazon